..................................................................................

# SURVIVING OR THRIVING?
## Managing Change in Housing Organisations

**ANDREW HOLDER, WENDY McQUILLAN,
ALF FITZGEORGE-BUTLER and PETER WILLIAMS**

..................................................................................

Chartered Institute of Housing
Policy and Practice Series
in collaboration with the
Housing Studies Association

**The Chartered Institute of Housing**
The Chartered Institute of Housing is the professional organisation for all people who work in housing. Its purpose is to take a strategic and leading role in encouraging and promoting the provision of good quality affordable housing for all. The Institute has more than 13,000 members working in local authorities, housing associations, the private sector and educational institutions.

Chartered Institute of Housing
Octavia House, Westwood Way
Coventry CV4 8JP
Telephone: 01203 851700
Fax: 01203 695110

**The Housing Studies Association**
The Housing Studies Association promotes the study of housing by bringing together housing researchers with others interested in housing research in the housing policy and practitioner communities. It acts as a voice for housing research by organising conferences and seminars, lobbying government and other agencies and providing services to members.

The CIH Housing Policy and Practice Series is published in collaboration with the Housing Studies Association and aims to provide important and valuable material and insights for housing managers, staff, students, trainers and policy makers. Books in the series are designed to promote debate, but the contents do not necessarily reflect the views of the CIH or the HSA. The Editorial Team for the series is: General Editors: Dr. Peter Williams, John Perry and Robina Goodlad, and Production Editor: Alan Dearling.

ISBN 1-900396-7-69

*Surviving or Thriving? Managing Change in Housing Organisations*
Andrew Holder, Wendy McQuillan, Alf Fitzgeorge-Butler and Peter Williams

Published by the
Chartered Institute of Housing © 1998

Cover photograph by Alan Dearling.

Printed by Cromwell Press, Wiltshire.

# Contents

# Preface

This book has taken some while to produce. Conceived in a tea break on a Strategic Leadership Programme at Pentre Gwylm, Cardiff, it has taken many months to get the ideas onto the screen. Managing the time to do research and writing has been the greatest challenge for the authors and they would acknowledge with great thanks, the patience and encouragement of Alan Dearling and John Perry. They would also wish to thank those hundreds of course participants and clients who have helped refine the materials which have gone into this book. We hope they like the outcome. Although a team effort, Wendy led at the front but Andy and his staff did a great job pulling it altogether at the end.

Finally, while the trio of freelance consultants, Andy, Wendy and Alf can give open rein to their view, Peter would wish to make clear that he has contributed in an individual capacity and nothing in the book should be seen to reflect the views of either the Council of Mortgage Lenders or the Housing Corporation.

**Andrew Holder, Wendy McQuillan, Alf Fitzgeorge-Butler, Peter Williams.**

# CHAPTER 1:
# This thing called change!

**Objectives**
This chapter introduces you to the book and:

- it explains why we have written the book;
- it offers guidance as to the structure of the book;
- it sets out the ways you might use the book.

## Introduction

Housing organisations have been subject to almost constant change in recent years. Ask any group of housing workers, whether front-line members of staff or chief executives/directors of housing, if they have had to cope with and manage change they will all say "yes". The front-line worker will talk of procedural changes, changes in reporting lines, new emphasis on things such as performance measurement and using new computer systems. The senior manager will talk about changes forced upon them by legislation or financial constraints, new organisational forms and directions.

Certainly the pressures all housing organisations have faced seem to be different in both scale and nature from those faced say ten years ago. Pressures for change have come thick and fast and from a range of directions, and these pressures have been felt throughout organisations. The incremental approach to coping with change that may have worked in the past, i.e. changing a little at a time, no longer seems as appropriate or even adequate.

None of this is unique to the housing sector or indeed to the public sector. All other public services and all private industries have had to change rapidly and fundamentally in response to economic, technological and at least as important, radical policy changes introduced by the UK's previous government. The fact that fundamental change has been required has often meant that previous experience and approaches had less relevance simply because the situations being confronted were so different. The change of government might have been thought to lead to a return to a more comfortable past. In practice, this does not seem likely. The new agendas being established may flow from a less negative stance to local government or public intervention but they are still framed with the context of limited resources. Themes such as value for money, targeting and competition remain important alongside newer concerns such as partnership, strategy and co-ordination. Change continues apace!

This book aims to help managers tasked with the challenge of guiding and shaping their organisations to best cope with, and exploit, the myriad fundamental changes they are faced with. It seeks to make sense of the changes which are taking place and to establish ways in which managers can assess the importance of the external and internal forces at work within organisations, their possible consequences and the ways organisations can adapt and respond strategically to change.

## The origins of this book

There is no shortage of books and articles on strategic and change management and many of those involved with housing have benefited from reading the works of the so-called 'management gurus', as indeed we have. Many managers in housing have asked, do these theories apply to housing? Can we apply private sector models to public sector? Is there something unique about housing which affects the manner in which it should be managed?

The book is written for those working in housing organisations. This is not to say it has no relevance to other types of organisations but it is written and informed by the experience of working with a wide range of housing organisations. All the authors have a background in organisational analysis and training and with the running of programmes devoted to strategic management and housing organisations.

It is this experience which has formed and shaped this book. In particular it was the development and running of the Chief Housing Officers' Programme (CHOP) at the School for Advanced Urban Studies, University of Bristol, the Leadership and Strategic Management in Housing (LSMH) course at the University of Wales, Cardiff, and now the Strategic Leadership in Housing Programme (SLHP) at the University of West of England which informed the overall structure and content. Through the successive running of the programme and its constant refinement it became apparent that there was a core of material and experience which could be distilled into a book which might have wide appeal and relevance. About 150 serving housing staff from a wide range of local authorities, housing associations, quangos and government departments have been 'through' CHOP, LSMH or SLHP. The participants have in turn taken back the experience to their organisations and applied it there. And as it has rippled out so that experience has fed back to the programme.

The book is in part, an attempt to answer some of the questions which have arisen over the years and to put in one place a collection of ideas, techniques and guidance for managers in housing who have to lead or manage organisations facing fundamental change. We hope it is a book for the practitioner rather than the academic, although we have included some theory when it is helpful to the understanding of the situations in which organisations and managers find themselves.

Over the recent past we began to see that there were some specific issues, concepts and management tools that were helpful and of practical use to managers facing the challenges of leading and managing changes in housing organisations.

The book is intended to be of practical help to managers who wish to initiate change themselves leading or being part of the change process. We therefore have suggested exercises and activities which will help the reader in this process, and have included very short, we hope 'digestible' summaries at the end of each chapter.

## A framework for change

We have evolved, with the assistance of many of our programme participants, a model or framework for change that managers can work with in a practical way. The framework offers a mechanism to examine the situation they and their organisation are in, and ways to assist managers develop the organisation and themselves in a positive direction. We have attempted to share this framework with the reader, putting it in a housing context and wherever possible illustrated with practical housing examples.

The framework is one way of bringing together all the various aspects involved in managing a major change. It is clearly not the only way, there are many books setting out other ways of doing this, but our model has a tried-and-tested quality which has worked for many housing managers.

The framework has nine elements each framed as a question (Figure 1.1). Three elements consider the strategic position of the organisation:
- What are the external forces for change?
- What are the internal forces for change?
- Why must we change?

Two elements consider how the business operates in its current and future positions:
- Where are we now?
- Where are we going?

Four elements consider the specifics of how the change is to implemented:
- What specifically needs to change?
- What specifically needs sustaining?
- How do we get from here to there?
- Where am I in all this?

**Figure 1.1: A framework for organisation change**

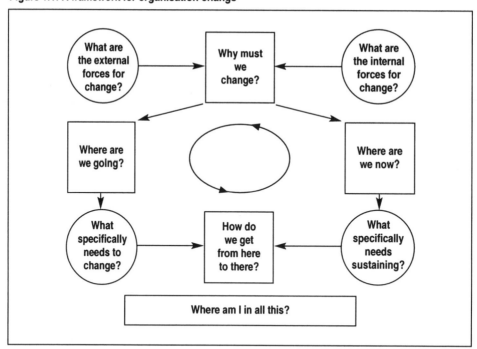

## The scale of change

It is important to be clear that although this focuses on the management of change, there are different levels. There are perhaps two important points of clarification to make.

## Operational or strategic change

First, the scale of change can be seen as a continuum, from operational changes to strategic change.

At one end of the continuum there are changes to be managed (in relation to the whole organisation), such as a change in procedure or of personnel in a team. We see this as an operational change, it still needs planning and managing but the change is about improving or re-adjusting the present state in the organisation, in a way very similar to the incremental changes we are used to dealing with. The change could be small and its significance limited to only one part of the organisation, or it could be large but not affecting the direction or nature of the organisation, e.g. a relocation of offices needs a great deal of management effort in managing a potentially disruptive change but the essential functions, nature and direction of the organisation remain the same as before.

The other end of the continuum would be a strategic change affecting the whole of the organisation in terms of the way it functions, its direction, culture or values. Often this is a large-scale change, e.g housing management compulsory competitive tendering (HMCCT) or large-scale voluntary transfer (LSVT). Equally it could be a relatively small change, but one which affects the whole culture of the organisation and the way it works, e.g. undertaking an initiative such as Investors in People, or changing the allocations policy in a way which will have implications for the management of the properties, void levels, repairs and future development.

We have used the terms operational and strategic to define either end of the continuum. Of course, a series of operational changes may add up to a strategic change, but not necessarily, the key being whether it affects the overall direction or nature of the organisation.

## Degree of control

Second, a further key issue is the matter of control; how much control an individual manager or the organisation has over the change? Most organisations have a high degree of control over changes such as introducing an IT system or in restructuring. However, there are other changes that they will not be in full control of, for example, changes needed as a response to community care will often need joint working and co-operation with other agencies. Similarly, managers in local authorities or associations who have to manage a change which affects or conflicts with the corporate working of the authority or association may well feel they do not have full control over the changes taking place. This would certainly have been the case for some housing departments in the recent local authority re-organisation.

The degree of control in any change is obviously a key factor in managing that change. However, it is just as important to know where and how you need to influence, negotiate and collaborate with others to achieve the desired outcomes.

We bring these two continua together in Figure 1.2.

**Figure 1.2: The scale of change**

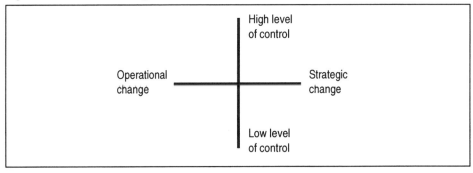

As a manager of change it is important to ascertain the nature of the change you are managing, i.e. where you would place it in the diagram above. We believe that managers in housing will always have to address, plan and manage strategic changes alongside operational changes in their organisation.

We have tried to address both strategic and operational change. We argue that managing strategic change demands a rigorous approach to analysis and thinking before embarking on implementing change. In which case we suggest that you at least consider the contents of all chapters. There are then some processes which apply to managing change of any scale, and which apply to operational or smaller changes. If you are managing these types of changes then possibly Chapter 4 and certainly Chapters 5, 9 and 10 will be appropriate. When reference is made to the whole organisation, this will need translating to division, unit or team.

Thus, although this is a book which addresses the management of strategic change, the skills and techniques applied will be appropriate to change management at all levels.

## Using the book

Each chapter addresses a particular element of the framework we have outlined and as far as possible follows the logical progression we have discussed. We recognise that the reality for many is a world that is not so logical, where change often stops and starts, and is interrupted or changes direction. This is more often than not a consequence of working within a system subject to national or local political pressures rather than being related to the way we manage. However, in the social housing sector, we must learn to live with these uncertainties, working with them as opposed to ignoring them.

Bearing all this in mind we have chosen to progress through the framework in a logical sequence. However, we would hope the format is such that the book can be dipped in and out of as the need arises, and that each chapter can 'stand alone' if necessary. For instance, the manager faced with implementing a change, can go directly to Chapter 9. 'How do we get from here to there?', rather than having to examine strategic issues first. We would of course argue that in order to implement change most effectively, an understanding and influence on the strategic process is important. However, we also realise that organisational life is not often based around the ideal!

Every housing organisation is affected by external factors including legislation, local and national policy on housing, finance and social issues, environmental, demographic and structural issues; the list is long. In every organisation the strategic planning process should include an appraisal of external factors and their particular effect on the organisation. Chapter 2 explores this external environment and its general effect on housing organisations, both currently and in the future. It attempts to map out those factors which are critical for managers in housing to understand and consider in their planning processes.

Within every housing organisation there will be a wide range of factors which are forces pushing for change. These may be inadequate systems or procedures which are inhibiting performance, particularly of individuals or groups who wish to develop new services; lack of resources; policy changes, or even a new senior manager wishing to make their mark. Chapter 3 considers these factors and their relationship to strategic planning and management in the organisation.

It is easy to see how many people working within the housing world feel that they have been part of constant change, and that the change is unremitting. Many see these changes as imposed and unavoidable. Chapter 4 considers 'Why must we change?' This chapter explores the necessity for finding a convincing and compelling reason to change. It also challenges the idea that an organisation must respond to every demand made of it, suggesting that there is some choice for the organisation in what it responds to as well as how it responds.

Subsequent chapters address the processes involved in managing change. In Chapter 5, the importance of understanding the strengths and weaknesses of your organisation is explained and techniques and tools to help gain a full picture of its current health are set out and explored. Following the work of the chapters on change (Chapters 2 to 4) and 'Where are we now?' (Chapter 5), there is a need to formulate a picture of where you want to be, i.e. being clear about the end result you are aiming for. Chapter 6 looks at how to do this, particularly in the current climate, where it appears at times as if the goal posts are constantly changing.

Chapter 7 explores the issues involved in sustaining the rest of the organisation in the midst of change, ensuring that the strengths remain strong and do not wither and perish from neglect. In managing change, managers often become 'change junkies', totally absorbed in the changes and often seeking further change when the current one begins to be implemented. Of course, the vast majority of staff in the organisation are concerned not with the change but with delivering the nuts and bolts of the business, keeping services running, and ensuring the organisation continues its core functions.

'If it ain't wrong don't fix it', is an old adage which includes a grain of truth. Knowing what to change is the key to the process, being specific about those changes and what outcomes are expected. Chapter 8 looks in more detail at this process of what needs specifically changing and what sustaining.

Having established where you are now and where you want to be, Chapter 9 addresses the issues involved in actually making those changes happen. It offers techniques and tools useful in change management and outlines the factors which need to be considered to enable any change to be successful.

The final box in our framework diagram is explored in Chapter 10. 'Where am I in all this?' considers your role as a player in the change, what personal changes you may have to make and how to cope with them. It offers exercises and tools to help you think through and survive as a manager and as a individual affected by change.

In many ways this chapter is the most important chapter in the book, for we believe that successful change is a result of what you do. You can carry the most erudite of theories and models in your head, know all the key issues and techniques but without self-awareness they may as well remain on the bookshelf. You need to know the impact you have on others, your style, your strengths and weaknesses. Only then will you be able to do the most appropriate thing for you, those around you and your organisation. Ultimately management is about choosing the most appropriate course of action in the particular circumstances and that choice will be unique on every occasion because of all the variables.

Hopefully this book will assist you in making choices and will be of practical help for anyone wanting to increase their understanding of the practical issues involved in trying to sustain and develop housing organisations in the current challenging environment.

It is offered as an aid rather than as a blueprint which must be followed to the letter. Every organisation and every manager does things slightly differently and there is no one way to achieve a desired outcome. Managers must have the confidence of their own abilities and should not feel that they must rely totally on a book or books to guide them. This book and the framework, the techniques and the analysis are there for you to draw from and to reflect upon. If it acts as a stimulus to better strategic management and helps managers and housing organisations to be more successful in their endeavours then it will have succeeded.

## Where strategic and business plans fit: a postscript

We should not proceed as if there is already no strategic planning or management framework in place. Most organisations will have one or more mechanisms for planning change, often recorded in planning documents such as business plans, operational plans, strategic plans, work plans and HIP statements. Close examination reveals that these documents vary considerably in their content and purpose. At the end of the day, of course, it does not matter what you call your plan, as long as you and everyone involved is clear about its purpose and how it will be used.

We would argue that any plan whose purpose is to establish the long term direction for the organisation, i.e. a strategic plan, should have considered the elements in the top half of the diagram, 'Framework for Change' (Figure 1.1).

In such a plan there should be an understanding of the current state of the organisation, and a full consideration of both external and internal pressures for change. Only then can the direction of the organisation be established and the reasons for that choice of direction.

A full discussion of these issues is contained in Chapters 2 to 6. The strategic plan would not normally be the plan to use as a working document to aid the organisation in making the changes. Business plans or operational plans are probably more suitable vehicles for establishing the detail of how the organisation will move from where it is now to where it wants to be. Work plans may be very specific, task-focused documents driving each area. There is of course some overlap between the different types of plans.

Business or operational plans should have considered in detail the lower half of the 'Framework for Change' model, clearly identifying the current state of the organisation, including not only the obvious areas such as performance and financial strength, but also culture and management style. Establishing the precise changes that are needed, and importantly the elements that need to be sustained in the current organisation and carried through to the 'new' is essential. Most importantly they should show how the organisation will move from the current state to the new. Another CIH publication, *Business Planning for Housing* (Catterick, 1995) offers more detail on this subject area. Work plans carry this implementation phase even further with detailed and regularly updated task-based programmes of work. These flow from the higher-level plans and can be cross referenced to them but the focus is on action.

Unfortunately, many organisations do the thinking, write the documents, then put them on a shelf to gather dust. While the process of producing such reports can itself be very valuable in terms of team building, clarifying objectives, building partnerships etc., the worth of such documents is in the use to which they are put. Business or operational plans should be the basis on which teams and individuals schedule their work and establish their objectives and targets (which might be enshrined in formal work plans as described briefly above). In this book we have not discussed the plan processes as such, although much of what we do talk about is fundamental to them. Where relevant we refer to other literature which can help put together both strategic and business plans.

## Further reading

Catterick, P. (1995) *Business Planning for Housing*, Chartered Institute of Housing, Coventry.

# CHAPTER 2:
# What are the external forces for change?

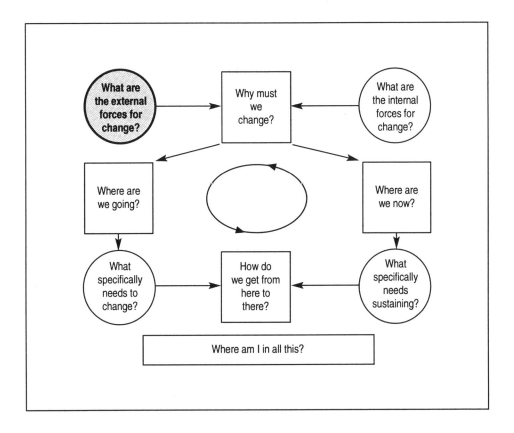

**Objectives**
This chapter will assist you to:

- recognise and understand the main external forces for change;
- analyse these forces within the context of your own organisation.

## Introduction

All housing organisations operate within a social, economic and political environment and must cope with the pressures and forces emanating from that environment. Chapter 2 sets out a broad overview of the primary forces bearing down upon housing organisations in Britain. It seeks to critically assess the impact of these forces and to consider the extent to which they are faced by all organisations. The focus is upon external forces for change. This then leads into Chapter 3, where we look at internal forces derived from the dynamics of the organisations themselves. An understanding of both external and internal forces is crucial to the process of strategic management because they form the overall environment within which your organisation functions.

## What is external?

Given this structure, a sensible starting point is to ask, what is external? As can often be the case there is always a tendency to explain the reason for any action as being, 'we had no choice', and by implication, 'we are not to blame'. Although we can define external forces as being those pressures which are derived from outside the organisation, the organisation itself contributes to the overall context within which those forces operate. So, for example, it may be that one external pressure is on wage control and the organisation had, along with others, in the previous year made a wage settlement well in excess of inflation. Equally, it could be a new government policy on void property introduced at a time when the organisation has a large number of vacancies. There is a question here of cause and effect and the multi-layered reality of any issue. Perhaps a more sensational example would be policy changes at central government triggered by over-publicised innovations at local government level designed to 'get round' government policy.

Just as there is a tendency to draw comfort from the fact that the pressures for change are purely external and out of the control of your own organisation, so too there is a temptation to see them as overwhelming and unstoppable. Although we use the term external 'forces' they are perhaps better described as pressures or tendencies because in some cases they are not overwhelming or unstoppable, even though it may appear so in the first instance. There can be no doubt that the immediate reaction to impending change is a combination of rejection and resigned acceptance. This stance can then be reinforced via both formal and informal discussions within the industry as many engage in condemnation and denial of a probably half understood reality.

Some may decide that this external force or pressure will have limited impact upon their own organisation and although they support the industry reaction, they recognise that they can live with the new issue (or even exploit it, as has been the case with the minority of authorities, who have voluntarily tendered their housing management functions under housing management compulsory competitive tendering (HMCCT)). By contrast, once the initial shock has been absorbed, others will decide they can get round the issue or that they will resist and seek change. The former has been true of local authorities who realised they could become *de minimis* within the original rules for HMCCT, while others working through the local authority associations have continued to press for amendments. Thus, when we think about external forces bearing down upon organisations we must recognise that they will have differential impacts. Some of us and our organisations will see them as more threatening than others. Given these differences this may raise questions about how your organisation can protect itself better from the external forces. Or whether it can exploit the changes and secure competitive advantages? The history of housing organisations in recent years is that there have been many initiatives which exploit policy change. In the local authority sector these have included large-scale voluntary transfer (LSVT), area renewal, tenant management organisations (TMOs), voluntary housing action trusts (HATS), and in the housing association sector, the use of cross subsidy, the generation of surpluses and the use of allowances.

It may well be that such pressures might encourage change but they might not require it, at least immediately. The threat of externally imposed change can trigger rethinking and restructuring even before it is needed. Here again we must recognise that the threat of an external force can be used to resolve an internal 'problem'. In that sense, externally imposed change can be **positive** because it can create the opportunity to tackle problems which were otherwise likely to remain unresolved, at least over the short term. This may relate to a wide range of issues including organisational arrangements, staffing levels or indeed key policy developments. The run up to HMCCT has been a case in point with some district auditors reminding authorities of the difficulties they may face in a tender competition thus leading to action on internal arrangements. Similarly, in some local authorities, there has been considerable resistance to the idea of local housing companies, not least from members. However, the creation of the Estates Renewal Challenge Fund and the signal that, whatever the government, companies were a favoured option, has forced members to think again. This has allowed officers an opportunity to consider the issues without political risks.

To conclude, we should not view external forces for change fatalistically and we should recognise that first, there will be differential impacts and second, within constraints, there will be choices. Finally, change may bring opportunities to address problems which would otherwise have remained untouched or been dealt with much more slowly. As is evident elsewhere in this book, the negative can become a positive.

## External forces for change

So what then are these external forces? The immediate reaction of many would be to say 'the government'. If only it was that simple, then perhaps, with the change of government it might all go away. In reality we now realise this is not the case. Government is but one, albeit a key one, of the range of pressures upon social housing organisations. Having a clear understanding of the shape and direction of external forces is a key requirement in the process of strategic management.

Perhaps the first task is to list out the main external pressures upon housing organisations and then go on to examine them in some detail. In broad terms there are perhaps four main external forces for change. These are as follows:

- changes in the economy;
- demographic and social change;
- changes in government policies;
- the local context.

Each of these broad pressures bears down upon housing organisations and produces pressures for change in structures, processes and procedures. Clearly they are all interlinked and it may at times be difficult to separate them out. Moreover, such is the gradual nature of change it may be that at times the forces at work will be hard to identify. A specific policy change by central government may be the first signal but on examination it might be found this in turn has been triggered by changes in the economy or more generally in society. It is important to analyse the difference between 'cause' and 'effect'.

## Changes in the economy

A range of macro-economic issues such as interest rates and employment trends bear down both on organisations and the individuals they serve. Shifts in interest rates can undermine the capacity of an organisation to service its debt and reduce its ability to respond to new housing needs and pressures. While most organisations should be able to manage this interest rate risk, the experience of the housing market recession revealed the extent to which individual households were unable to service their individual debts. In part, this was because of both rapid increases in interest costs and the onset of increased unemployment, but it also clearly revealed how the general economic environment can bear down upon the fortunes of individual households, just as in the early 1970s the high rate of inflation forced changes in the housing finance system. But solutions can become problems, as in the case of fixed rate and deferred interest structures introduced in order to cope with high inflation and rising interest bills, which can become a problem when general rates are falling and the organisation is tied into arrangements which reflected previous pressures. Financial risk management has become a central feature of housing associations in the era of private finance.

The general health of the economy has a huge impact upon housing organisations and of course on central government. Government might be forced to cut public expenditure and while housing organisations rely on public expenditure in one form or another they are vulnerable as a consequence. It is very noticeable that government capital expenditure on housing has been reduced much more sharply than other programme areas.

Beyond impacts upon central government and the transmitted consequences to local organisations, changes in the economy have a wide range of other effects. They not only impact upon the resources housing organisations have available to meet needs, but at the same time they can increase the demand for those services, via increased homelessness and reduced access to other tenures. They can impact upon the price they must pay for materials and labour and potentially open up the market for rival organisations who can compete through greater efficiency (derived perhaps from being part of a larger group and a willingness to cross subsidise).

While there can be no escape from the economy it should be clear that organisations vary in the extent to which their existence will be threatened by it. This is because of differences in relation to factors such as the following:

- reliance on grants or permission to borrow;
- structure of borrowing;
- level of staffing;
- use of technology;
- number and cost of offices;
- overall efficiency.

All of these factors will be significant influences on the scale of the impact of pressures emanating from the broader economy. An organisation which has relatively few offices, low staffing and makes good use of technology might have greater flexibility during periods where there are high wage pressures than one which does not. This may appear to be a very modest example of the effects of the economy. But the point has already been made that there will be major effects on the overall structure of demand and supply and it is important to recognise that these lower level, yet nonetheless important outcomes, exist. At this level managers can exercise control. They can take strategic decisions to 'insulate' their organisations from pressures from the economy as far as is possible. Loan debt is another obvious example. A judicious balancing of fixed and variable rate money spread between short and long terms may give an organisation a degree of protection which another organisation reliant upon a single type of loan structure will not have.

## Demographic and social change

Quite clearly, there have been important changes in the structure of the population and households. Overall the population is ageing with reductions in the number of births (down from 963,000 per annum 1961-1971 to an estimated

703,000 per annum by 2021-2031), and increases in the number of deaths (639,000 per annum 1961-71 to 693,000 by 2021-2031). Migration is a further important factor with, for example, the South East losing 16,000 people in 1994 and the South West gaining 24,000. Equally there have been important changes in the number and structure of households. There are now more single person and single adult with children households, while the number of two parent with children households has been declining. Projected ahead it is predicted that the number of single person households will increase sharply.

However, it is important to recognise that such projections are very vulnerable to assumptions about the rate of household formation and household migration. As a number of distinguished commentators have argued there is a circularity in household projections and housing provision (Murie, 1976; Bramley, 1996). The more housing that is built the more households can form, and the more that form the more pressure there is to build homes. Demographic change and migration trends in particular are also vulnerable to influence from changes in the economy. The recent housing market recession has resulted in households delaying the start of a family while migration is strongly influenced by the health of regional and national economies as households make long distance moves.

The fundamental shifts in the demographic structure are echoed in changes in society and the community. There has been a growing fragmentation of society and residualisation and exclusion of certain groups within it. Partly this is a product of shifts in the distribution of income and wealth. There has been both greater equality as measured by the rise in the number of households with above average incomes and assets, while at the same time the gap between them and a smaller group has widened, reflecting greater inequality (Hills, 1995). As always, evidence regarding changes in the distribution of income are contested. The Department of Social Security (1996) recently analysed the situation over time and argued that there was little evidence of a growing group of individual households who had got progressively worse off in income terms over the last twenty years. This was because there was movement through the system. At the same time the Institute of Fiscal Studies (1996) published an important study showing how social housing tenants, as a group, have become ever more marginalised over the last decade or more. Moreover there has been a deterioration in the financial returns to employment faced by social tenants. An increasing dependence on means tested benefits has increased out-of-work incomes relative to in-work incomes (ibid, p.127).

For housing organisations, these changes bring a number of pressures including:

- increased demand from households without the resources to command alternatives in the housing market;
- increased poverty amongst their clients with reduced capacity amongst households to secure employment and an adequate income;

- increased management and other costs;
- reduced public support and sympathy for both the poor and those organisations which house the poor;
- an erosion of 'community values' and an increase in individualism and 'anti social' behaviour.

All of this can then find expression in the so-called 'degrees of difficulty' in the management task. Success can become more elusive not least because the range of issues to be confronted becomes so wide. A narrow approach to management might be justified on the basis of the defined task and the paid for service, but this can result in the neglect of other factors which contribute to the likelihood of 'success'. However, although there is now a widespread recognition that 'housing plus', i.e., wider housing role and activity is a valid and necessary goal, there remains the question of who pays for it.

## Changes in government policies

The joke question, 'why is housing policy like the No 9 bus?' and the answer, 'because another one will always be along in a minute', or, 'because they come three at a time', is part and parcel of the housing scene. Since 1979 there have been at least 18 major pieces of housing legislation. Change has become a watchword for housing organisations not only in relation to the broader social and economic context, but also in the substance and detail of the policy framework in which they operate. This has been brought into clear focus by the change of government. Prospectively the government's 1997 comprehensive spending review (CSR) of housing may be the launching pad for a range of new policies. Regardless of that, since coming to power the government has announced a number of initiatives. These include:

- the phased release of local authority housing capital receipts;
- the announcement of the replacement of HMCCT with a new regime of Best Value (but the continuation of HMCCT until that comes into being);
- the exploration of extending the private finance initiative to Housing Revenue Account homes;
- encouraging lower rents in the social rented sector not least via the introduction of 'rent controls';
- not proceeding with some planned restrictions of housing benefit;
- amendment of homelessness regulations introduced by the previous government;
- in Wales, the abolition of Tai Cymru, the quango responsible for funding and regulating housing associations. In Scotland, Scottish Homes will be reviewed while in England the position of the Housing Corporation has been reaffirmed.

Regardless of the detail of these new initiatives it is evident that policy change has come at housing organisations on a number of fronts. These include:

- social housing policy including HMCCT and homelessness legislation;
- local government re-organisation;
- home ownership including reductions in mortgage interest tax relief and income support for mortgage interest;
- the promotion of private renting;
- the erosion of housing benefit and related welfare support;
- changes in taxation;
- a wide range of policy driven changes in the housing and mortgage markets.

It is important to recognise that policies stemming from parts of the government other than the Department of the Environment, Transport and the Regions (DETR) can be of crucial significance. The role of the Department of Social Security is well recognised because of housing benefit just as is that of the Treasury. However, policies emanating from the Home Office have recently been important with respect to refugees and the Departments of Health, Education and Employment have all initiated policy with housing outcomes, e.g., through training schemes or work for unemployed youth there is an effect on homelessness, while increased fees and student loans means young adults enter the housing and labour markets with an existing debt. The shift towards private health insurance and the pressure on care costs may result in some households struggling to pay rent or maintain their homes.

The wider impacts of policies stemming from other parts of government on housing is now widely recognised and the government is seeking to build links between departments so that they can be better evaluated. The same is true of the wider effects of housing policy and the DETR has been quick to point to the wider benefits of housing expenditure (for example on jobs, health and educational achievement). As a reflection of this, the Housing CSR has involved over 30 officials from 5 departments plus Wales, Scotland and Northern Ireland and a range of specialist units and agencies within government.

Without doubt, most housing practitioners could identify a series of policies introduced in to the 1980s designed to diminish their role. The list of policies is given on page 18.

There have been a number of clear dimensions to policy proposals, much of which was directed to local authority housing. First, the aim was to enhance the choice and power of tenants to exit the sector (as both owners and as tenants, but also through choosing to join other organisations). Second, if tenants chose to remain with local authorities they were given greater control over their landlords via rights to repair and a much more formalised process of consultation, state management boards and tenant control. Third, the resources available for local government housing were reduced so that new build became marginal and then

**Table 2.1: Principal housing and related legislation, 1979-96**

| Legislation | Main housing policy elements |
|---|---|
| 1980 *Housing Act* and *Housing (Tenants' Rights, etc.) Act, Scotland* | Introduced 'right-to-buy', Tenants' Charter and New Housing Subsidy System<br>Changes to Rent Acts |
| 1980 *Local Government Planning and Land Act* | Changes to Local Government Finance (England and Wales) |
| 1982 *Social Security and Housing Benefits Act* | Established Housing Benefit System |
| 1984 *Housing and Building Control Act* | Extended and tightened 'right-to-buy' |
| 1984 *Housing Defects Act* | Obligations placed on local authorities in respect of sold defective dwellings |
| 1985 *Housing Act* | Consolidating |
| 1985 *Housing Associations Act* | Consolidating |
| 1985 *Landlord and Tenant Act* | Consolidating |
| 1986 *Building Societies Act* | Enabled building societies to own and invest in housing directly and to compete with other financial institutions |
| 1986 *Housing and Planning Act* | Increased 'right-to-buy' discounts (but Lords' amendment excluded dwellings suitable for the elderly)<br>Facilitated block sales of estates |
| 1986 *Social Security Act* | Modifications to the Housing Benefit Scheme |
| 1987 *Housing (Scotland) Act* | Consolidating |
| 1988 *Housing Act* | Deregulation of private renting<br>New financial arrangements for housing associations<br>Tenants' Choice and Housing Action Trusts introduced (England) |
| 1989 *Local Government and Housing Act* | New local authority rent and subsidy systems<br>Changes to urban renewal policy (England and Wales) |
| 1990 *National Health Service and Community Care Act* | New arrangements for care in the community as alternative to institutional/residential care |
| 1993 *Leasehold Reform, Housing and Urban Development Act* | Enabling leaseholders to acquire freehold interest in their property<br>Rent to Mortgage Scheme |
| 1996 *Housing Act* | Changed duties on homelessness and allocations; new powers to create 'introductory tenancies' |

almost impossible and all remaining resources had to be concentrated on upgrading and repair of the existing stock. Fourth, the basis upon which local authorities were financed was changed so that they became ever more dependent upon capital receipts and rental income. The latter was offset against the housing benefit entitlement. Rents were pushed up by the government thus increasing benefit dependency in the hope that as near market rents were achieved it would be easier to encourage tenants to leave the sector or to attract other landlords in. In the event, the rising benefit bill has forced government to back off from this strategy and now a low rent strategy is seen as being beneficial.

This strongly negative environment encouraged some authorities to accept the option of leaving the sector. Via large-scale voluntary transfer the authorities have transferred their stock, typically to a new housing association set up under . their auspices. The authority gets a capital receipt on sale of its stock, the association can borrow to buy the stock from the local authority. So far over 56 local authorities have gone down the LSVT route and around 250,000 homes have been transferred out of the local authority sector. It has been a broadly successful policy in that new investment has been levered in to finance the upgrading of the transferred stock and for new building outside the constraints of public expenditure controls.

It is evident that most of the authorities which have transferred their stock have been in Conservative controlled shire districts. LSVT has not been a major force in the larger Labour controlled shire or metropolitan districts. Partly this is a question of ideology, partly the economics of the deal (in many cases the association receiving the stock would have to get a large dowry from the authority to deal with catch-up repairs), and partly pressure from tenants and members not to go down this route. The Labour government is seeking to address these issues because it too recognises the merits of transfers.

LSVT has posed a difficult question for housing organisations. Some chief officers supported it because it offered a prospect of a regime free of political involvement and restores a sense of control which has been reduced in recent years. It also offered valuable opportunities for staff to transfer to the new organisation and to gain new career paths.

The previous government set in place arrangements to allow the creation of local housing companies (LHCS). These companies would be similar in effect to LSVT transfers except the LHCS could be more strongly local authority 'influenced'. With a change of government it is increasingly evident that most authorities are now adopting a 'wait and see' strategy with respect to future plans. However, there is considerable momentum behind LHCS and it is now certain some will now emerge. The £320 million Estates Renewal Challenge Fund (ERCF) made available by government to encourage this initiative was substantially oversubscribed and further rounds of ERCF support have now been announced.

Fifth, through the disciplines of compulsory competitive tendering of housing management, the local authority would be forced to prove that it was offering a cost effective service. Many authorities had been working through the 1980s to enhance the quality of their service and its efficiency and effectiveness in response to customer, member and officer demand, pressure from the Audit Commission and because they were keen to maximise the use of the resources available to them. HMCCT has been seen to bring benefits in terms of a range of disciplines and new competencies, but it has to be seen in the context of a central government view that for the most part the authorities were inefficient and expensive. HMCCT was one further way of removing them from the equation. Once again, however, authorities have proved themselves resilient and capable of meeting the challenge. So far HMCCT has not proved to be the final hurdle at which the service would fall.

The focus of this discussion has been upon local authorities and the transfer process. This is one good example of where crucial strategic issues are being confronted. There are others. Housing associations have had to face up to a reworking of the financial regime they operate under. The move to private finance and much greater competition for grant funding has brought forward major issues about the future viability of individual associations. This has triggered strategic reviews related to whether to continue developing, to diversify, albeit with appropriate risk management, to afford themselves of opportunities which might arise under HMCCT or LSVT and, of course, whether to expand through mergers and perhaps create group structures, or indeed to transfer to another association. The future has been seen as sufficiently complex and hostile that all options have been considered. The pace of change in that operating framework (which now includes 'rent controls' and issues about the use of reserves) has meant that all developing associations have had to review their future on a regular basis.

It is little wonder that whatever the merits of specific pieces of legislation and some of the ideas and concerns embedded within them, housing organisations have felt under siege. While morale has been lifted by the continuing 'success against the odds', there can be no doubt that local authorities have had to face and overcome the problems of both the circumstances of their tenants (and the deterioration in the general environment in which they operate), and a continuous and corrosive pressure from central government.

Finally, in terms of policy we can no longer ignore the European Union (EU)! It is evident that although the EU has 'delegated' responsibility for housing policy to the national governments it does have a growing role in the broad area of housing. This comes about in a variety of ways. For example, through other policy areas such as competition, industrial development and social policy. Competition policy impacts upon the conduct of CCT and the letting of contracts. EU industrial and social policy is concerned with ensuring EU residents have reasonable opportunities for employment and full access to health and education facilities. To achieve this it has often been necessary to assist with the provision of housing since it is through a stable address that residents can access such opportunities. As a consequence, housing organisations now need to pay ever greater attention to EU activity both because of regulations, but also the resources which can flow via EU programmes (see Chapman and Murie, 1996, for a useful review).

## The local context

In all of this it is important not to neglect the local context. Outwardly, authorities and associations may each appear similar to other authorities and associations. It is very tempting to suggest that all will respond in similar ways to the same stimuli. But in reality they don't and they won't. Each organisation has its own history, economics and politics. This will influence officers, members and its users.

It is very clear for instance that many households have had a long term relationship with the local authority as landlord. They have no wish to transfer to a new landlord and to move from the familiar to the unknown. While their current landlord may not be perfect many will be only too aware of the failings of other landlords. And in the case of the local authority they have a councillor to back them up and demand change when needed.

The local context will also influence the degree of exposure to alternative structures and processes and the extent to which there is competition for staff, resources, tenants and local power. It means that there will be a series of unique responses to events and circumstances. It is this localism which potentially gives great strength to organisations in that they are best placed to identify and respond to local issues. But as is clear in so many other contexts, given the right pricing, quality and promotion it is possible for other outcomes, and organisations to penetrate this local monopoly. Local context therefore is a powerful factor but it must be respected rather than taken-for-granted and abused. Finally, as we argue in the next chapter all organisations have a dominant culture and style. This will impact upon the way it responds to change.

## How to take stock of external forces

Given that each organisation is probably facing a unique constellation of pressures, it is important each undertakes its own assessment of the forces bearing down upon it. While it is possible to start with the generalised analysis set out above this should be the starting point rather than the end of the analysis. Moreover, as will become evident in the process, different parts (and people) of the organisation will see and experience those pressures in different ways.

There are a number of ways of assessing external forces. One is to commission internal or external consultants to undertake a strategic review. Another and perhaps more formal mechanism is to set up one or more staff groups to undertake a PEST analysis (Grundy, 1993).

PEST stands for political, economic, social and technological. These are seen as the generic forces of change and the question is, using these headings, set down what you see as the main pressures upon your organisation (or part of it). This might be undertaken as a rapid brainstorming exercise or it could be the product of a longer seminar, perhaps facilitated by an external advisor. A PEST checklist is appended (Table 2.2). This should simply be seen as one list. Your brainstorming might suggest other factors which should be added to the list (or deleted from it) – see also the list at the beginning of Chapter 6. Once the list has been generated you can debate how important each factor is. This will then give you a list of key factors to consider and to track over time.

**Table 2.2: Political, economic, social and technological (PEST) analysis**

**How may political and regulatory change impact on your service?**
- What new national political interventions are likely?
- Is it likely that Best Value and other government policies will substantially reshape the housing sector and, if so, how and over what period?
- What other regulatory changes (legal, environmental, safety etc.) may shift 'the rules of the game?'

**How may economic and financial changes impact?**
- How are economic cycles (i.e., growth/recession) likely to affect the way in which you manage major change?
- How are financial markets and services likely to affect what you can do, and by when?
- How is public expenditure, particular for housing, likely to change, and when?

**How may social and demographic changes impact?**
- What social trends exist which may reshape the values and behaviour of customers, and thus, how service demands are met?
- What social trends exist which may reshape the way in which people do business in the housing sector.
- Does your strategy reflect changes in demographic patterns, for instance in the number of people in particular age groups, their purchasing power and changing life styles?
- What are the specific demographic trends in the geographic area(s) where your business has greatest concentration?

**How will technological change impact on your strategy?**
- What new or emerging technologies may reshape your industry?
- Who will be the leading players in exploiting this technology?
- Will the transformation be slow and incremental or will it be more sudden and revolutionary?
- Will the greatest impact of technology be through:
  - internal processes?
  - external relationships to customers ?

(Adapted from Grundy (1993))

Equipped with your list one can then begin to start to frame the strategic responses. As it is often said, if you don't know what forces you are responding to how can you plan for the future? Establishing the forces for change is part of the process of working out where you are coming from and where you might be going. Clearly there is no point simply listing those forces that are evident now and in the past. It is important to think about how these pressures may change in the future and what new pressures may emerge.

It will not be possible to anticipate everything! The world does change in ways we cannot anticipate. Moreover, factors that were seen as less important might become much more important. All you can do is to give it a go and make a best approximation. Returning to the list annually or every time you review plans will allow you to gauge how well you had predicted what might happen.

## Summary

The external environment is very important and should be not be neglected. Understanding how it impacts upon your organisation and how that environment might change is a vital step in the strategic management process. Regardless of how big or small your organisation or where it is located these external pressures bear down upon it (and your competitors!).

In thinking about how you might wish to see your organisation change and develop it is important to understand and anticipate the pressures which you will have to face from external forces. As mentioned above some of these pressures may have a bigger impact upon your competitors (who may also be less well prepared) and as a consequence could open up opportunities for your organisation. A well run organisation is one which will anticipate change, adapt to it and exploit it to advantage. Even if your plan is to stand still, you will probably have to change in some ways to remain the same overall!

---

### Checklist of points

- All housing organisations are effected by forces which emanate from the external environment.
- These forces include changes in the economy, demographic and social change, policy change and the local context.
- These external forces are constantly changing in terms of their shape, direction and influence.
- Although the external environment is complex and constantly changing, simple techniques can be used for analysing it.

---

# Further reading

## (a) For techniques:

Beckhard, R. and Harris, R.T. (1987) *Organisational Transition: Managing Complex Change*, Addison-Wesley, Wokingham.

Catterick, P. (1995) *Business Planning for Housing*, Chartered Institute of Housing, Coventry.

Grundy, T. (1993) *Implementing Strategic Change*, Kogan Paul, London. This is a very helpful guide to practical techniques for handling change. The PEST analysis is described under Environmental Analysis (p.111).

## (b) For understanding trends in the wider housing environment:

Bramley, G. (1996) *Circular Projections*, Rural Development Commission.

Chapman, M. and Murie, A. (1996) 'Housing and the European Union', *Housing Studies*, 11, 2, 307-318.

Clapham, D. (1996) 'Housing and the Economy: Broadening Comparative Housing Research', *Urban Studies*, 33, 45, 631-648. A recent review article on this topic.

Giles, C. et al. (1996) *Living with the State: The Incomes and Work Incentives of Tenants in the Social Rented Sector*, Institute of Fiscal Studies, London. A timely and helpful study of how the population of tenants in the social rented sector has changed.

Glass, N. (1995) *Housing and the Economy*, Harry Simpson Memorial Lecture. This is a useful overview of housing and the economy from a government official (now at the Treasury).

Hills, J. (1995) *Income and Wealth*, Joseph Rowntree Foundation, York. A current and helpful guide to the distribution of income and wealth.

Malpass, P. and Murie, A. (1994) *Housing Policy and Practice*, 4th Edition, Macmillan, London. A text book but valuable for bringing it all together and giving a longer term perspective on the way policy etc. has changed.

Murie, A. (1976) 'Housing Need, a Circular Argument', *Housing Review*. An old but useful article of the circularity of projections/needs studies.

National Federation of Housing Associations. (1996) *Economic Forecasts for Association Business Plans*, NFHA, London. An invaluable annual guide to trends over the next four years. Useful for both associations and authorities.

Wilcox, S. (1997) *Housing Finance Review 1996*, Joseph Rowntree Foundation, York. This is an invaluable compendium of housing related data over a run of years.

# CHAPTER 3:
# What are the internal forces for change?

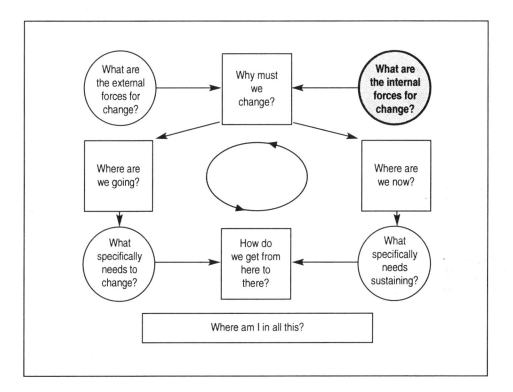

**Objectives**

This chapter enables you to:

- recognise and understand some of the important factors which underlie the internal forces,
- recognise and understand some of the primary internal forces for change;
- be able to analyse and map internal change.

# Defining the relationship between external and internal forces of change

The previous chapter defined internal change as, *"forces which are derived from the dynamics of the organisation itself."* (Chapter 2). These internal forces for change will now be the focus of discussion here. It is, however, important to bear in mind, as already suggested, that the concepts of 'external' and 'internal' change are sometimes difficult to disentangle. It is also arguable that, since perceptions of the need to change and what action to take emanate from the observations and ideas of individuals within an organisation, who in turn are influenced by external factors, most change is external in origin. One example is the rate of technological change. New technology has transformed communication within our society (Beckhard and Harris, 1987, p.11) and must obviously be categorised as an external factor. But a new computer system might also be the result of internal change – the perceived need to manage information more effectively or to network between different, perhaps decentralised, work stations throughout the organisation. Clearly, one could not have one change without the other. Another example might be councils who have engaged in Voluntary Competitive Tendering, which although resulting from an internal, often a political, decision, was made possible by the Local Government Act 1988 and the subsequent extension to housing management.

The distinction between external and internal may be somewhat blurred; no organisation is insulated from the external environment, but there are some forces for change which **appear to be** internal in origin. Accordingly, for the purposes of this chapter and to assist the analysis, internal change will be defined as change which arises from either the paid members of an organisation or from others (such as committee members or housing management contractors, say, under HMCCT), who are so closely connected with a housing organisation that they must be considered to be an integral part of it.

# Underlying factors affecting internal change

There are some underlying organisational factors which might help us to understand how internal pressures for change arise. What is meant by the term 'underlying factors'? Broadly, these may be seen as organisational conditions which tend to bring about, or are necessary for, internal change. Six conditions have proved to be critical to internally generated change:

- the extent of political or managerial leadership (as change agents);
- the occurrence of key decisions in the recent past or near future;
- the extent of the supportiveness of the organisational culture;
- the extent to which change has been, or is being, planned;
- the need to improve efficiency;
- perceived obstacles to effective organisational functioning.

These will now be discussed in turn. Firstly, **the importance of change agents at a senior level** (senior managers and the political leadership) should not be underestimated. It is at this level that internal response to external change is generated. Secondly, the **occurrence of key events** *"which had a catalytic effect in transforming management philosophy"* (ibid, p. 23) has also been mentioned in the literature. When considering the housing sector specifically, such events might be the decisions leading up to Large Scale Voluntary Transfer (LSVT), or setting up a Local Housing Company, or a significant organisational review which leads to de-layering and/or job losses.

These first two underlying factors are also linked to a third; the **extent of support for change in the organisational culture**. The term 'culture' as applied to housing organisations is comparatively new but can be summed up as, 'how things are done round here.' One major problem with this concept is that it can mean everything and can easily be reduced to a meaningless word. It can be helpful with the analysis of internal change forces since here we are referring to organisational culture – the patterns of behaviour of managers and staff within an organisation. Cultural analysis is a way of attempting to understand why managers and staff act as they do, then considering whether such behaviour is appropriate (and supportive of an organisation's values and aims) and, if it is not, attempting to do something about it (easier said than done).

However, when thinking about the patterns of behaviour within housing organisations, it is important to consider some basic organisational types (forms) which may be found within the sector. Fitzgeorge-Butler (1992, Chapter 1, p. 5) refers to three basic types – autocratic, bureaucratic and participative, but other authors such as Handy, have referred to power (autocratic), role (bureaucratic), task/network and person cultures (1976, pp.178-185). Whatever typology is employed, there are some key factors underlying organisational cultures, which tend to determine their patterning.

One of these is 'management style' and there may be a dominant style (and correspondingly a dominant culture) within housing organisations. The reason for this is the simple rule about 'following my leader.' Organisational management styles develop according to the style being exhibited by the head of the organisation. If the leader tends to consult, then a participative type of organisation will develop. There is also the question of the function of the organisation, or the different elements within it – a different culture will necessarily develop around rent arrears collection, compared with, say, a tenant participation team (their functions are different). But, broadly, housing organisations will have one dominant style.

Examples of cultural changes which have occurred in recent years include:

- customer-driven approaches;
- cost-driven approaches such as HMCCT, of which activity-based costings became the prime instrument;

- reducing the managerial layers within housing organisations (increasing empowerment and personal responsibility of staff);
- responding to our multi-cultural society more effectively by monitoring the fairness of access to jobs and services;
- quality assurance schemes (satisfying customer wants and needs, with given resource parameters);
- the development of Best Value, which reintroduces quality considerations into the cost/quality equation.

It is, however, widely recognised that it is **culture change** which is required to deliver excellent services, continuous improvement, and best practice, not solely the measurement and auditing of services.

Fourthly, Baron and Greenberg have distinguished between **planned** and **unplanned** change and applied this to external and internal forces (1990, Third Edition, Table 2, p.563). They commented that a great deal of organisational change comes from a conscious decision (planned change) to alter the way an organisation does business or the very nature of the business itself. For example, there have been, and are, forces impelling housing associations to either merge with, or to take over others, by way of rationalisation within the industry. Such decisions are internal, in the sense of being decisions by one association to take action, but also external, in that it necessarily involves another organisation. In time this leads to internal changes due to the need to harmonise policies, procedures, practices and operating norms. One change leads to other internal changes and highlights the possible effects of changing the services offered and the administrative systems, as part of a planned strategy.

The different forces of internal change, and the levels at which they happen, may also determine whether the change is to be planned or not. One of the key differences between internal and external change is that it is more likely that internal changes will be planned since they are not forced on the organisation, rather they are conscious and rational decisions by managers, or others, to change. Time for planning can therefore be found. The approaches to, and techniques of project planning and management are of particular relevance here since they can provide practical planning methods (see Burton and Michael, 1992)

Internal change may be 'evolutionary'; continuous, incremental, but unplanned because it largely goes unnoticed. This is more likely at the small and medium scale levels. Over time, such apparently small scale change may add up to change, which is altogether more substantial. Additionally, large-scale change must be, or at least should be, planned because of its wide ranging nature and the ramifications it will have for the whole organisation. This might be regarded as 'revolutionary' change – the 'big bang' effect.

Fifthly, it was very common for changes in administrative systems to be strategically planned in advance and as such changes may stem from **a desire to improve efficiency** (Baron and Greenberg, p.564). They also characterised performance gaps as being unplanned in the sense that when they come to light, an unanticipated organisational response is required. Grundy (1993) also made a similar point saying internal change might come about through the recognition of "performance dips." (p.54).

Lastly, perceived **obstacles to effective organisational functioning** will also provide evidence of the need for internal change. Most senior officers are all too aware of internal pressures, and the need, for change, but some are also facing internal resistance to change. Some common difficulties **may be** as follows:

- acceptance of mediocrity – the 'it's more than my job is worth' mentality;
- little or no concept of best practice;
- rejection of new ideas;
- a 'blame' culture which reduces risk-taking;
- managers and staff undermined by committee members;
- lack of management training;
- lack of basic management and financial information;
- little incentive to improve services;
- self-serving (enclosed) attitudes;
- negativity;
- cynical and obstructive attitudes;
- lack of basic customer care;
- lack of strategic direction.

Some of the above are serious impediments to progress and may themselves be seen as forces for internal change.

These underlying changes are usually linked in that one may suggest the need for change in another aspect. Management styles largely define organisational culture; overly bureaucratic cultures may lead to ineffective functioning, and so on.

These general approaches to underlying change factors are useful for beginning to clarify the types of changes and challenges facing housing organisations. They also assist with an analysis of why housing organisations must, or want to change, and to what forces they are reacting and what the internal consequences will be.

The following example clearly demonstrates that these underlying factors must be satisfied and resolved before change can take place.

## Example 3.1: Housing Association: underlying factors affecting the forces for internal change

A medium sized community-based organisation (about 1200 general and supported housing units) had been formed largely at the instigation of one man and a small number of like-minded people, who subsequently formed the committee. Decision-making was by consensus, which clearly had absorbed a lot of time and energy. Problems began to arise in terms of a lack of clear goals and objectives; but the organisation ran reasonably well until it began to seriously expand in the late 1980s. It was under pressure from the regulatory authority to spend HAG, but also the Director had reservations about the kind of properties which were being built – a question of them not always meeting the needs of customers in terms of design and location. As the Development Section expanded, it become a powerful force within the organisation – it became a development-driven organisation.

As the Association expanded, the management style of the Director changed too, from seeking consensus to a more authoritarian style, which ran counter to the expectations of many staff who had joined the Association in the early days. There was no open revolt about this change, which had been brought about by the need to establish some kind of hierarchy with a clearer decision-making structure, but rather a simmering pot of discontent, which had no outlet other than in rumour, gossip and rising levels of personal dissatisfaction. Poor performance was allowed to persist, especially in the Development Section, and the regulatory authority intervened to curb the lack of policies and procedures, the inattention to rising rent areas and to improve the, generally perceived, poor management of the Association. It was widely felt that the organisation had outgrown the capacity of the Director to manage it. Change was clearly required but the Director remained to block any significant change. One consultant had been engaged to attempt to resolve the difficulties within Development but this had been ineffective. But soon after there were drastic cuts in HAG and the Development Section was pretty ruthlessly cut – some staff were dismissed, others were re-deployed throughout the organisation, adding to the previous feelings of discontent. Additionally, the committee took no action, probably out of deference to the founder figure and a lack of reliable information about the true state of affairs.

Eventually, the Director left and a new one was appointed with a clear mandate for change.

This organisation was perceived to be ineffective in that people were clearly unhappy about the change of culture and lack of commitment and motivation. The regulatory authority was also unhappy about poor performance (an external force), and the need for change was obvious. But effective action was blocked by a powerful figure within the organisation and until this block was removed little effective action could be taken.

The above example raises some important issues about the degree of choice with respect to change, especially since internal pressures for change are sometimes overlooked, dismissed or ignored. Senior managers are likely to have more control over any internal factors driving change (Beckhard and Harris, 1987, pp. 33-44), but external pressures are much more difficult to dismiss. It is therefore possible that overdue internal change may only be tackled by housing organisations when they are forced to address such changes in the face of powerful external forces. The imposition of compulsory competitive tendering is a good example of this since it ensured that councils in particular were obliged to apply more business-oriented approaches. Similarly, housing associations had to respond as lenders requiring evidence of sound organisation and business planning.

## Analysing change: SWOT analysis

After you have considered the underlying factors, a powerful tool for bringing together the internal forces for change is the SWOT analysis. This commonly used analysis tool identifies the organisation's strengths, weaknesses, opportunities and threats (SWOT). It has a dual function – of identifying the internal forces within the organisation and providing appreciation of external factors but from the perspective of internal members. An illustrative example is provided on page 32. A much more thorough analysis will be achieved through the preparation of a Capability assessment (see Chapter 5).

It will be noted from the SWOT analysis below that factors can be both an opportunity and a threat, as well as weaknesses and threats. The team which completed this had a good appreciation of external funding threats as well as the need for support from the wider organisation. A SWOT analysis can provide information about a very extensive set of issues. It is also possible that a further SWOT analysis might be required to clarify particular forces for change. Grundy (1993) provides a particularly interesting example in which a Management Team analysis identified broad issues such as market technology, regulatory trends and competitive activity, all of which were subject to considerable uncertainty. It was subsequently felt necessary to make a further analysis of these key strategic issues from the specific point of view of competition within the sector. This had the effect of moving some strengths into the weaknesses column and some weaknesses were re-classified as strengths. Some care must be exercised with respect to choosing the correct perspective, since it is intensive analyses such as these which provide clues about the effectiveness of the organisation and the importance of the individuals' perceptions and feelings.

Having mapped the various forces for change in the SWOT analysis, a Force Field analysis, described in Chapter 9, is a useful tool for assessing how to deal with them. In particular it can identify how to build on strengths and minimise the weaknesses.

**Table 3.1: SWOT analysis**

| STRENGTHS | WEAKNESSES |
|---|---|
| Committed staff | Under considerable pressure |
| Teamwork | Over stretched |
| Sense of humour | Lack of office cover |
| Flexibility | Constant answering of telephones |
| Swift reactions | Need more training |
| Good management style | Isolated |
| Small teams | Lack of support from senior managers |
| Feeling of 'togetherness' | Unclear roles |
| Other team members' accessibility | Rising rent arrears |
| Allowed to use common sense | Computers don't always work |
| Good communication | Lack of air conditioning (concentration) |
| Use individual strengths | Not a balanced patch |
| Few men (men don't listen) | Staff hard to replace |
| A mature team | |
| Good training | |
| **OPPORTUNITIES** | **THREATS** |
| Develop good practice | New methods of working (redundancy) |
| Extra IT skills | Old guard within the organisation |
| Make a name for ourselves | SHG rates |
| More personal development and learning | Tenants sometimes |
| Developing organisation | Lack of IT support |
| New methods of working | Key staff leaving |
| The organisation can learn from us | Lack of senior management support |
| | Rent arrears |
| | Lack of policies and procedures |

# Major internal forces for change

It is however clear that there have been some major internal forces for change affecting the housing sector in the 1980s and 1990s. The following section deals with a number of these, namely: decentralisation; listening to customers; the enabling role and 'fitness for purpose'; strategic thinking; new methods of working; and the introduction of competencies, skills and knowledge through National Vocational Qualifications (NVQs). Each force is dealt with in turn.

# Decentralisation

This trend to decentralise or localise services has affected local authorities and housing associations alike. It began with the setting up of area offices in the 1970s, and has subsequently been perceived in the 1980s and 1990s as a sensible mainstream practice (Burns et al, 1994, p.4). They point to two important meanings of decentralisation:

(1) The physical dispersal of operations to local offices.
(2) The delegation or devolution of decision-making authority to lower levels of administration.

It is also closely connected with other notions such as 'getting closer to the customer' (see the publication by that name, LGMB, 1987), whereby local offices facilitate a greater understanding of the needs of a particular locality, and to the question of 'accountability' (more a political imperative for local authorities, than housing associations). However, it is easier to set up local offices in an area, which is geographically relatively compact and bounded, as is the case with local authorities or associations which work in one specific location. Conversely, it is much more difficult for a more widely spread organisation, where some of its power to decentralise will be lost.

There is no doubt that this trend has been, and will continue to be, a powerful force for internal change. With decentralisation comes the need to devolve budgets, authority and ultimately real power. This is clearly envisaged under Best Value approaches (see Fitzgeorge-Butler, 1997).

It has also brought particular problems in its wake, such as possible feelings of isolation, and the difficulties of communication between offices and between the periphery and the centre. This, in turn, can create power struggles about who exercises ultimate control. To work effectively, there needs to be clarity about the meaning of, and what is being offered by, decentralisation, including the scope of delegated decision-making. But clearly, one of the major changes associated with decentralisation is structure.

A decentralisation strategy can unleash powerful forces for change upon an organisation. Senior managers may have addressed the need to change the structure but many other aspects of the change can still require resolution. There is need for a structure but also an appropriate culture and network of interpersonal relationships, associated with a decentralised structure. Accordingly, it is prudent to attempt to anticipate what these problems and difficulties might be before attempting the change and the provision of solutions. It is very important to analyse the nature of the change being undertaken and its intended consequences. Getting the structure right is therefore only one aspect of change, and may not be the most important aspect

## Listening to customers

The idea of getting closer to customers has already been mentioned and is one of the most important goals of decentralisation. This goes hand in hand with involving and consulting customers about the housing services to be offered and how those services are to be delivered. However, within the housing sector this has tended to be by means of passive methods of consultation such as customer satisfaction surveys and complaints procedures.

Housing organisations also have to be proactive in their attempts to consult, involve and encourage the participation of customers. By this means services can be better targeted and geared to real needs, which can be delivered in the right quantity at the right time and place. The need for authorities to develop approaches to Best Value will mean that even more participatory methods will be required.

The corollary of this approach is that housing organisations will need to find out what customers want from the organisation and its services, and attempt to provide it. A customer-focus is a key value to be pursued by managers and staff and be written into the organisational aims and policy. This change has come about because of external factors: recent government requirements (Best Value); better educated tenants; rising expectations fuelled by consumerism (no deference is expected at the local supermarket); disenchantment with impersonal bureaucracies and the failure of public bodies to deliver sufficient housing services.

Clear and published performance standards and targets may ensure that housing officers are held accountable for their actions. Services may also be delivered more informally, with easier access and this has been encouraged by greater decentralisation. Contact with the public can be more positive and better information can be provided to encourage customers to apply for the services they need. Although produced in 1987, the LGMB publication, *Getting Closer to the Public* has many good practical ideas by which this may be achieved.

What methods might be used to achieve essentially customer driven, continuous improvement to service delivery? Macgill and Beaty (1995) point out that action learning is based on learning from experience with two key stages; reflection upon issues and problems, and action (p.32). Housing managers must use methods which are inclusive, and have the capacity to involve all sections of the resident community, especially those who are perhaps particularly vulnerable or liable to social exclusion.

## 'Enabling' and 'fitness for purpose'

The above discussion assumes that housing organisations are the direct providers of services and the concept of the 'enabling' organisation presumes that housing organisations, especially local authorities, encourage other organisations to provide housing and related services. This has been characterised as working with and through a variety of agencies and organisations to meet housing needs

(Stewart, 1988, p.21). More recently this approach was further defined; *"local government should only do those things that the private sector cannot do"* and *"not a direct provider of services, but rather as the enabler arranging for others to do the work"* (Hender, 1993, p.3).

This idea is also related to the twin concepts of a market ideology and a pluralistic system of service provision, where public housing organisations only provide what the private sector cannot. Again, while these ideas emanate from outside housing authorities and associations, they are being forced to respond to them, or at least, in the case of housing associations, to encourage more and more private finance to fund their activities. The ever diminishing role for local authorities is outlined by Goodlad (1993).

These developments have had a knock-on effect, and enormous implications, for the shape of service provision. For example, all housing staff need to develop cost-conscious attitudes, and to generally run housing organisations more like businesses. The extension of Compulsory Competitive Tendering to housing management has given a massive impetus to this, as has the need to satisfy lenders that an association is being run effectively. Such a change cannot be achieved practically without spending time and effort educating housing managers about business methods, such as the use of Management Information Systems, the notion of managing a service rather than administering it, and how to reduce costs and maximise income whilst maintaining quality. The moves to develop new methods of working include making greater use of the telephone and less visits, customers reporting repairs directly to contractors, and one-stop housing shops. Some of the above methods have been borrowed from the direct banking and insurance sectors.

In short, housing organisations must be 'fit for their purpose', which presumes that they know what their purpose (and direction) is. But what does this term really mean? In terms of public management, 'fitness for purpose' was applied to the new challenges facing local authorities in the early 1990s (LGMB, 1993). It developed the ideas of organisations being clear about their strategic direction (and the way strategic choices are made) and their role in terms of community leadership and strengthening public involvement and accountability. It also stressed the importance of effective decision-making processes and the application of efficiency, effectiveness and equity to local authorities. Connections were also made between notions about the learning company/organisation and the need for authorities to learn and change as a result of learning. By the application of these ideas, an organisation could be made fit for its purpose, thereby achieving its overall strategic direction and goals.

It has a wider application to housing organisations because of the range of 'dominant roles' which could be adopted: direct service provision; maximising the use of the private sector; co-operating across a wide range of other organisations (what is now termed the 'inter-agency' approach); and devolving more power to communities. It is clear that some of these roles may be applied directly to housing organisations: the big city housing departments; departments which encourage the involvement of the private sector; housing associations which operate within a network of agencies and partners; housing departments and associations which encourage high levels of community and tenant participation. These were, however, only developed as illustrative models as to how key assumptions and strategic choices could shape a dominant role for a particular organisation. The above models were then used to work out certain organisational implications for each and also key organisational issues. This approach demonstrates that it is the blend of external and internal influences which really shapes organisational form and affects, in turn, the internal functioning of the organisation in terms of the roles of committee members, senior managers, the administrative centre, the pattern of relationships with other agencies and organisations, relationships with the public and management and staffing arrangements. Perhaps one of the key lessons coming out of the fitness for purpose debate was the need for a clear strategic direction.

## Strategic thinking

There are links here to housing managers adopting a strategic attitude and way of thinking when considering organisational responses to the forces of change acting upon their organisations continually. This is linked further to the idea of strategic management, which involves (after strategic planning/business planning has taken place), the identification of key issues and developments, those which will require substantial changes to the structure and functioning of the organisation (certainly large-scale *not* small-scale change). Some changes are more obvious: Large Scale Voluntary Transfer; setting up a Local Housing Company; merging with another organisation; and Local Government Review. These developments have entailed managers thinking in strategic terms about what is best for their customers, and led management teams and committee members into making important choices about the future direction of their organisations. The examples cited above are a mixture of changes emanating from both external and internal forces. All but merger requires external sanction and even this may require regulatory approval. Moves towards a more customer-oriented approach within housing organisations have, however, provided an opportunity for changing their organisational culture and two aspects of strategic management are important here – managing change and culture change (see Fitzgeorge-Butler, 1992, for a fuller discussion of the dimensions of strategic management).

Strategic thinking is about considering 'the big picture'; analysing, and planning for substantial change; identifying the key priorities; developing the organisation as a whole; providing leadership at a strategic level; encouraging middle managers and staff to perform at the highest possible level (requiring motivation and firm commitment); implementing the corporate/business plan and the associated change processes; and evaluation, monitoring and review of the preceding activities.

In terms of internal forces for change, we have already met the Director, whose organisation outgrew them (Example 3.1), and it can be seen that what is appropriate in one context will not be appropriate for another. It must be emphasised that a single leadership, management style or culture is wrong but appropriate styles/cultures will depend on what the organisation is setting out to achieve and what it has to do to achieve it. For example, if a housing organisation has a key value of 'putting the customer first', or in terms of this chapter, getting closer to the customer (the driving force behind Best Value), then an autocratic style would be wholly inappropriate because autocracy tends not to listen to, or consult with, people. Rather, a participative or empowering style should be encouraged.

Such issues will almost certainly show up in a SWOT analysis as a weakness or strength of the organisation, or as a threat to its continued survival. In any event, apart from the management of crisis, autocratic styles of management are outmoded and counter-productive. The dominant values of society have changed somewhat and consequently staff expect to be consulted.

Therefore we reiterate that the perceived appropriateness of the culture is a very powerful internal force for change (and indirectly, so will be the dominant management style of your housing organisation). In other words a key question must be asked – is the culture and/or management style 'fit for its purpose?' The following exercise may assist you in assessing the culture of your housing organisation.

---

### Exercise 3.1: Analysing the culture of your organisation

(1)   How would you describe your organisation in a word or phrase?

(2)   How would you describe the current, dominant, management style?

(3)   What are the guiding principles or values which underpin your organisation?

(4)   Do you like/dislike working in your organisation? Why?

---

The kind of results one might expect from such an exercise obviously depend upon the culture of the organisation in question. If one looks at question 3, a range of answers is possible depending on either an explicit list of values in use or implicit values, in use but not consciously formulated. The danger with the latter is that this state of affairs allows negative values to flourish, which may run counter to the expectations and needs of customers. The culture (composed of, and determined by, the values in use) will not be fit for its purpose, namely the achievement of agreed goals and objectives. These results may run in parallel with responses to question 4, especially with respect to dislikes about working for an organisation. This question explores the individual's feelings about a given organisation, which will be based upon perceived effectiveness or ineffectiveness of the organisation.

Experience has shown that in expressing their likes/dislikes managers use such words as: 'crisis management; stress/pressure is ignored; complacency; lack of direction; lack of team spirit/teamworking; isolation of decentralised offices; standards and targets poorly monitored; and a lack of accountability and control'. These types of answers may then be related to what needs changing within that organisation. The overall effect of Exercise 3.1 will therefore have been to characterise the dominant culture, which can then be compared with the overall aims and objectives of the organisation. This can lead to questions like: Is this what we want? Do we need to change it?

## New methods of working

The application of new technology to housing management became more necessary as housing organisations decentralised their services. Neighbourhood officers require immediate and easy access to information held at the centre and in turn have the ability to amend records. This required computers to be 'networked' across all aspects of housing management – repairs; rent accounting; benefits and allocations.

Some housing organisations have also developed 'customer call' centres which, by their very nature, require up-to-date new technology. They also mark an important break with the principle that housing services are usually (and relatively expensively) delivered face-to-face. The origins of this change are in the development of direct banking and insurance services and with the need to cut costs generally. This development has been taken up particularly by housing associations which are not tied to service delivery in a particular locality. Such centres have also been used to call tenants in rent arrears during the evening time in order to advise them of how they might pay off their arrears.

New technology has also facilitated the collection of a wide range of information from each patch area and provided new methods by which tenants might access services, such as on-line information services.

One danger, however, is that such changes are made for the benefit of the organisation, rather than that of customers and it would therefore be proper to thoroughly research and consult with customers before the introduction of such wide-ranging changes.

# Competence, skills and knowledge

One aspect of the above analysis concerns the question of the competence of managers and staff, which relates to the scope and degree of the capabilities, the skills and the knowledge possessed by them. This relates to what is expected of them in order to carry out the aims and objectives of a particular organisation, which, in turn, connect to its values. Handy made the point that people (individuals) are important to any organisation, and especially (we suggest) to housing, where so much of the work with customers relies on dealing with customers face-to-face or on the telephone (Fitzgeorge-Butler and Williams, 1995, p.116.). Any lack of interpersonal sensitivity by managers and staff is quickly noticed and noted.

The coming of National Vocational Qualifications (NVQs) to Housing has given managers a valuable tool for both assessing competence and for closely identifying what further skills and knowledge are required by staff in order to be fully competent. This has been further extended through Modern Apprenticeship frameworks by which young people can be encouraged into the sector through pump-priming funding by local TECs.

A more conventional approach has been to undertake a Training Needs Analysis (TNA) of an organisation in order to identify and quantify skills shortages, which may also be weaknesses in terms of the SWOT analysis. The difficulty with the TNA approach is that it tends to identify a wide range of training deficiencies which are usually not prioritised in terms of the key needs of the organisation. For example, it may be undeniably useful for staff to enhance their knowledge of housing law, but if they spend most of their day dealing with the public then the priority must be to ensure that they have the essential skills and knowledge to carry out their key task. The question is not only what do individuals need, but more importantly, what does the organisation demand of individuals in order that the former achieves its aims and objectives?

It is clear that, whilst individuals are important, and rightly so, this must be balanced against organisational needs. The skills and knowledge deficiencies of individuals may therefore trigger the need for change (often glaring deficiencies arise as a result of changed organisational and/or role priorities). However, these should only be considered in the context of the strategic purposes and needs of the housing organisation.

One approach which attempts to balance personal and organisational training need is that of Investors in People (IIP). This approach has been called the ISO9000/2 for people and requires a public commitment to develop all employees, to achieve its business objectives, which are communicated to and understood by staff. Outcomes are also evaluated.

The process involves the following activity:

- action plans;
- statement of objectives;
- human resources (HR) policies;
- statement of HR policies;
- business plans;
- line manager development;
- understanding and application of NVQs;
- induction programmes;
- performance review and appraisal schemes;
- employee survey;
- accreditation.

One cannot quarrel with a system which assists with the provision of quality staff, who are aware of overall objectives and who are provided with high quality training to carry out their tasks.

---

**Exercise 3.2: Internal forces for change**

Review the internal forces for change within your organisation, using the factors raised within Chapter 3.

Questions to ask

(1)   What is the source of the internal pressure to change?

(2)   How is the need for change manifesting itself?

(3)   What kind of action is required?

(4)   What action is currently being taken?

(5)   Is it effective? How do you know? If ineffective, why is that?

---

## Summary and conclusions

We began this chapter by acknowledging the difficulties of disentangling the forces for external and internal change. It was then argued that there are some underlying factors which are important to understanding the functioning of organisations and which also assist with the categorisation of internal change forces.

It was suggested that it is also important to use tools, such as SWOT analysis, which can be used for the analysis of organisational effectiveness.

The discussion then turned to consideration of specific major forces for change such as decentralisation and 'listening to customers', especially since they have such significance for the new Best Value regime. Two further useful concepts for the analysis of internal change forces were then introduced, the 'enabling organisation' and the concept of 'fitness for purpose', which were also linked to the previous discussion.

The importance of strategic management was considered and it is now clear that the advantages of using it as a conceptual framework for an improvement of approaches to, and techniques for, the management of housing organisations seem advantageous. This was also linked to some of the tasks to be undertaken by senior managers, as they manage change strategically, and to the idea of cultural change – the changing patterns of behaviour within housing organisations. Promoting culture change is just one of the tasks of the strategic manager. Another task is ensuring that the organisation is equipped with competent managers and staff but this has to achieved within the context of organisational priorities.

This chapter has discussed the wide range of internal change forces through an analysis of the underlying and other factors at work and the specific issues which will face senior housing managers as they manage change. It also confirms the importance of considering external and internal forces of change together. Finally, it may be useful to address the question of the need for change in your own organisation.

# Further reading

Baron, R. A. and Greenberg, J. (1990) *Behaviour in Organisations: Understanding and Managing the Human Side of Work*, Allyn and Bacon, London.

Beckhard, R. and Harris, R. T. (1987) *Organisational Transitions: Managing Complex Change*, Addison-Wesley, Wokingham.

Bines, W., Kemp, P., Pleace, N. and Radley, C. (1993) *Managing Social Housing*, HMSO, London.

Burns, D., Hambleton R. and Hoggett, P. (1994) *The Politics of Decentralisation: Revitalising Local Democracy*, Macmillan, London.

Burton, C. and Michael, N. (1992) *A Practical Guide to Project Management: How to Make it Work in Your Organisation*, Kogan Page, London.

Fitzgeorge-Butler, A. W. (1992a) *Organising Change*, Absolutely Essential Management of Housing series, Milton Keynes.

Fitzgeorge-Butler, A. W. (1992b) *Strategic Management*, Absolutely Essential Management of Housing Series, Milton Keynes.

Fitzgeorge-Butler, A.W. and Williams, P. (1995) 'Quality and Social Housing: Irreconcilable Partners?' in Kirkpatrick, I. and Martinez Lucio, M. *The Politics of Quality in the Public Sector*, Routledge, London.

Fitzgeorge-Butler, A. W. (1997) *Best Value: A Strategic Framework*, Absolutely Essential Management of Housing Series, Milton Keynes.

Goodlad, R. (1993) *The Housing Authority as Enabler*, Longman/CIH, Coventry.

Grundy, T. (1993) *Implementing Strategic Change: A Practical Guide for Business*, Kogan Page, London.

Handy, C. (1976) *Understanding Organisations*, Penguin, Harmondsworth.

Handy, C. (1995) *Beyond Certainty*, Hutchinson, London.

Hender, D. (1993) *Managing Local Government Services*, ICSA Publishing, London.

Leach, S., Walsh, K., Game, C., Rogers, S., Skelcher, C. and Spencer, K. (1993) *Challenge and Change*, LGMB, London.

Local Government Management Board. (1993 a) *Fitness for Purpose: Shaping New Patterns of Organisation and Management*, LGMB, London.

Local Government Management Board. (1993 b) *Managing Tomorrow: Panel of Inquiry Report*, LGMB, London.

Local Government Training Board. (1987) *Getting Closer to the Public*, LGMB, London.

Macgill, J. and Beaty, L. (1995) *Action Learning* (second edition), Kogan Page, London

Stewart, J. (1988) *The New Management of Housing Departments*, LGMB, London.

Young, K. and Mills, L. (1993) *A Portrait of Change*, LGMB, London.

# CHAPTER 4
# Why must we change?

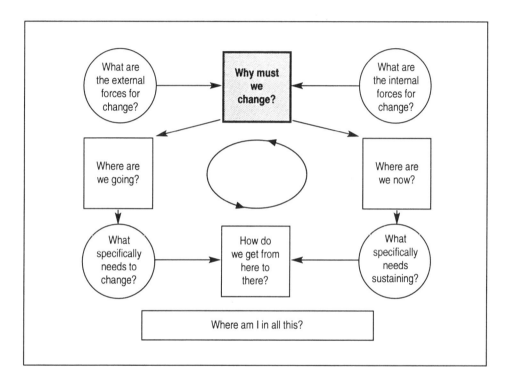

**Objectives**
This chapter will enable you to develop a convincing answer to this
question by helping you define your:

- *Starting point* — What are the specific triggers for change?
- *Analysis of the situation* — What are the critical factors and how
  are they to be investigated?
- *Support for the change* — What commitments are there from key
  stakeholders?

This should provide you with a thorough assessment which is a realistic
balance between the extremes of a lengthy study, for which a busy housing
organisation has all too little time, and an answer made up on the hoof.

# Introduction

It is one thing to be aware of the general forces acting on all housing organisations to change, as spelt out in the previous chapter. It is yet another thing to answer specifically the question of this chapter, 'Why must we change?' In other words what forces are relevant and what must be responded to. For your organisation to change successfully, it must have a convincing answer to this question.

The reason we stress this question, which at first sight seems obvious, is that the lack of a clear answer has caused many changes in housing organisations to falter. Failure to work hard at the 'why' of change before spelling out the 'what' of change has made the changes more difficult, and in some cases, less effective. The reasons for this failure are all too familiar:

- *The failure to analyse the need for change before rushing into specific solutions.* In this chapter, we set out some typical issues that trigger change and methods of analysis which are thorough without being excessively time consuming.
  **There is a need for adequate analysis.**

- *The failure to recognise that major changes affect the meaning and satisfaction that people get out of their work.* Most of those who work in housing value not just their pay but also the purpose of their work; namely providing social housing, and who they work with, namely colleagues with similar values. Any major change needs to explain why it is necessary and how it affects these valued aspects, otherwise it will appear merely meaningless and disruptive.
  **There is a need for reasoning and conviction.**

- *The failure by managers to realise that their familiarity with the reasons for change, gained through hours of discussions, is not shared by staff.*
  **There is a need for careful communication to staff.**

The organisation has only so much capacity to work and change. To carry changes through into practice demands hard choices, clear focus, much explanation, strong commitment, many resources of time and money and, not least, persistence. A convincing and specific answer to the question 'Why must we change?' is a crucial part of this process.

## The starting point – what are the triggers for change?

The start of any change must be some trigger, or triggers, which stimulate your thinking about change. It may be you have a sense of unease, have unfavourable comparisons with other housing organisations, or merely have read the previous chapter! It is important to be clear what these are because they shape the range of factors considered. As analysis proceeds, these factors may prove to be more or less relevant, but they provide the key for the initial assessment. What, in other words, is your starting point?

Where there are several triggers, then some priority must be applied. Igor Ansoff (1987), who has been influential in the development of strategic management, has argued that for any organisation to survive effectively, it must, above all else, match changes to its operating 'environment'. In other words, the environmental triggers for a housing organisation, e.g. its tenants, the local economy, its legislative basis and funding regime, *must* determine the services it provides *and in turn* the way it is organised. Ansoff argues it is in that order. It is not, as in some of our organisations, the other way around, internal pressures altering services and expecting the tenants and customers to respond accordingly. *Environmental forces should primarily determine changes in the organisation – it should be environmentally driven.*

A range of possible triggers for change that could affect you are:

**A rapid change in the operating environment.** This may result from a rapid decline in the local economy, such as industrial closures or communities suffering multiple deprivation and requiring a wider response than a housing response, such as employment or leisure.

**Rule changes**, either internally or externally imposed. As a local authority housing department, you may have to face Compulsory Competitive Tendering (CCT), when you previously expected to be exempt. As a housing association, you also have to respond to an annually declining grant rate which necessitates alternative funding strategies. Both may face a new duty imposed by the government to establish *Best Value* services.

The **lack of demand** for one aspect of the service through trends, market competition or unfavourable quality comparisons. A more radical approach rather than managing a steady decline might be needed. An example in one authority was of unlettable flats requiring radical changes either in the rules of letting or the rents.

An **unease expressed by a significant stakeholder** (interested party), e.g. the DETR expressing concern at the level of rigorousness of Best Value applied to the housing service or the Housing Corporation suggesting an amalgamation of two associations for longer term viability.

Some **internal procedure** of your organisation giving rise to serious dissatisfaction. An example of this might be the rent setting process, which is totally geared to political expediency, rather than the needs of the service.

The **latest trend in thinking**. Not perhaps a good reason on its own but sometimes a starting point which leads to a significant strategic shift, e.g. decentralisation, estate action, tenant participation, de-layering, group structures for housing associations, generic working.

A **timely moment to review** the organisation. This may be when there is a change of chief executive or chief officer, or there are changes on committees or other major changes which have an impact, e.g. Local Government Re-organisation.

**Unplanned changes that start** to happen, e.g. illegal tenancies that break rules that perhaps ought to be broken.

These and other factors may be the triggers for change. In order to draw them together, the writing of a position paper can be helpful (see Exercise 4.1). It is a means of bringing your thinking together and to establish your starting point. The clarity of your understanding of the change, as reflected by the position paper, is important for both designing *and* evaluating the effectiveness of the changes. It must lead, however, to a more thorough analysis.

---

## Exercise 4.1: Drafting a position paper

One straightforward way of collecting your initial thoughts is the following process:

1) Take an A4 sheet and divide it into three vertical column

| 1. TRIGGERS | 2. OUTCOMES | 3. IMPLICATIONS |
|---|---|---|
| List the various triggers or forces for change to which your organisation should respond. | Set out the outcomes you want for your organisation and over what time scale. | List your initial thoughts about the likely implications for the organisation (direct or indirect, positive or negative) if you do or do not make the change |

2) Initial ideas could be tested with your management group or a cross-section of staff.

3) A draft position paper needs to be written to make the case for change, based upon this *initial* thinking. This paper is not *the* case for change but will help crystallise the assumptions and identify the gaps which require more rigorous analysis.

4) Initial reactions to the paper (which may, because of sensitivity, be limited to a management group) can form a very helpful indication of what, and how much more, needs developing.

---

# Analysis of the situation – what are the relevant factors?

Your position paper will have identified the key changes that require a response. Many will be familiar; you will have familiar ways of analysing them, and, as likely as not, familiar ways of resolving them. In this section we offer four methods of analysis which may help you deal with the less familiar and more difficult changes. Three of them address externally-driven changes (following Ansoff's argument) and deal with:

- *The threat of competition.*
- *The challenge of comparison or the pursuit of Best Value.*
- *Unclear pressures which demand change.*

The fourth deals with change that may initially be driven by internal pressures:

- *The internal problems which are becoming intractable* and may threaten the organisation's future.

All four methods have been used extensively by senior managers from local authorities and housing associations who have attended our strategic management programmes. Whilst we would not claim they are easily applied – as many managers would agree – they have in many cases helped managers make sense of what they face and how to shape a response.

## The threat of competition: Porter's 'Five Box' model

Competition has been introduced into social housing in its three main areas:

- *Maintenance, management and development.*

Despite some expectations to the contrary, the *Best Value* regime will continue to place considerable emphasis on competition and testing services in the market place. In whatever way competition affects your organisation, it is crucial that your organisation assesses its competitive position and adopts an appropriate, strategic response. For those entering a competitive market the cost of providing a service to a set quality level may seem to be the only significant factor – and indeed this may turn out to be the case. However, there are often other tactical responses to competition that can legitimately be deployed, e.g. being open-ended on quality, and the packaging of contracts to make them awkward for the competition.

One systematic way of making this assessment which we have found particularly useful for housing organisations is Michael Porter's 'Five Box' model. A well respected writer on strategic management for the private sector, Porter has identified five main forces at work when an organisation faces competition. Importantly this is more than the immediate competition. Figure 4.1 sets these out, and they are:

A.  The *immediate competition* already competing over a particular product or service. This would be in housing development, management or maintenance. An example in the maintenance field would be local building contractors competing with the in-house maintenance organisation.

B.  *Potential entrants* who are ready and willing to *establish* themselves in competition, but are currently active in other fields. The CCT legislation has stimulated many companies to consider entering the housing management field, e.g. water companies, estate agencies, and facilities management companies.

C.  *Substitute services* which would replace the need for the product or service. An example would be when home ownership takes people out of the social rented sector.

D.  *Buyers, who are the end users of a service,* have some influence over the types of service and the competition through their buying power. Social housing has not traditionally given its 'buyers', i.e. tenants, much buying power. This is because of its monopoly position and complex, and separate funding (e.g. housing benefit) but customer care initiatives and increasing tenant involvement are shaping services and giving more power to its buyers. *Best Value* requires a strong involvement of buyers in policy, planning and monitoring.

E.  *Suppliers,* who provide the essential ingredients for the organisation to function. This can be as diverse as the government supplying finance and 'legislation', the local labour market providing staff, and other parts of a local authority providing legal and financial services. An example of the government's supplying power is that of cutting off most finance to development activity in the local authority; there is now a minimal presence in the field.

Whilst it is crucial for you to be aware of what competition is currently available (Box A), an analysis of changes in the other four boxes can give a more systematic and realistic picture of what it will take to compete successfully. Porter's valuable contribution has been to argue that an effective organisational strategy, *"takes offensive or defensive action in order to create a defendable position against the five competing forces."*

**Figure 4.1: Michael Porter's 'Five Box' model**

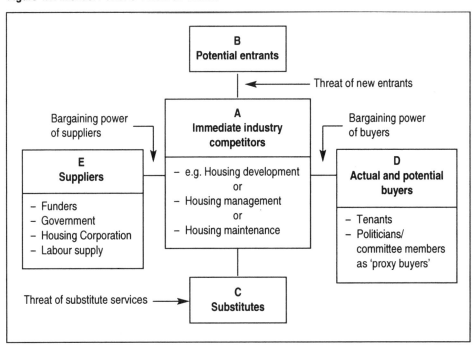

An illustration of its use in one local authority housing department may usefully demonstrate its use in practice. The department, facing CCT and at an early stage of preparation, decided to assess their situation using Porter's model. A simplified and adapted form of their analysis is described next and follows a process similar to that at the end of this section.

Figure 4.2 sets out their initial analysis. Starting with *Box A* there was little to go on because currently there was no immediate competition – they were facing the first round of CCT. Turning to *Box B* they knew, however, there was a range of potential entrants. There were the obvious names of companies operating nationally who had declared their hand, some regional housing associations who were making reassuring noises that they wouldn't compete (but would they?), and some local companies who might 'throw their hats in the ring'. At the time no estate agencies had shown any signs of interest. Indeed the department subsequently discovered that it was an incomplete and potentially changing list.

With *Box C* there were, at first sight, no immediate substitutes. The 'right-to-buy' had dried up and most tenants were either tied financially or emotionally to the council's housing. On closer inspection, three substitutes emerged: the possibility of large stock voluntary transfer (LSVT); invited external management (Voluntary Competitive Tendering without an in-house bid); and estate management boards. All would avoid the need to face CCT. The critical issue with all three was the time necessary to gear up. The political and tenant debate necessary to make the case and prepare for each of the three was felt to be too difficult and too time consuming given the deadlines.

**Figure 4.2: Housing management CCT**

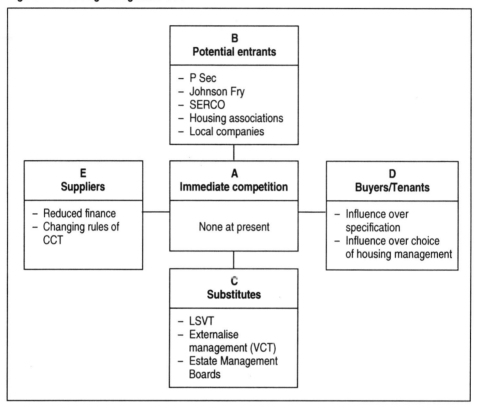

Recognising the necessity to face CCT, they completed their initial analysis. They had already begun to consider the likely views of the buyers (tenants) and, sometimes, 'proxy' buyers (politicians). Turning to Box D they identified what they knew of their tenants', (and to a lesser extent politicians') preferences and began to examine how they might influence the contract specification of the service and the choice of contractor. The department also examined ways in which suppliers, Box E, and notably government policies on housing and housing finance, might affect their future, which was felt to be both uncertain and possibly depressing.

The results of this initial use of Porter's model led the department to:

- recognise that they had to prepare for CCT;
- identify what further evidence they needed of potential entrants, their intentions and practices, e.g. what could be gathered about their

management practices, costs and bidding elsewhere (for VCT or other contracts)? The department was seeking this information and updating it until weeks before bids went in;

- consider packaging of services to deter the entrance of those who thought they knew housing management but would balk at other aspects, e.g. homelessness;
- examine rigorously their own costs in the light of early information from competitors and reduce them in preparation;
- identify more clearly tenants' preferences and, in response, which were crucial for the specification, highlighting awareness of current strengths of the service or adapting them;
- make a more thorough assessment of likely housing policy and housing finance changes over the next few years (inevitably a risky process).

The process was, for this department, a systematic way of considering the full range of factors in a competitive environment. It was subsequently used and updated, though in greater detail. It is a way of analysing and thinking through a competitive situation. An outline of the process is set out next in the form of a self-assessment exercise. It is clearly not able to deliver an answer by itself, but should help you do your own thinking, identify management follow-up, and identify a working strategy in a competitive environment.

---

### Exercise 4.2: Applying Porter's 'Five Box' model

We suggest that you take one aspect of your housing organisation's activities which are subject to competitive changes. This may be for the first time due to legislation, e.g. CCT or *Best Value* preparation of the housing management function in a local authority, or undergoing threatening changes, e.g. the reduced development grant rate from the Housing Corporation. Draw together a small group of knowledgeable managers – it may be your management team. Then carry through the following assessment. The level of detail and rigour may not be great initially, but it must raise the awkward 'what if?' type questions that are threatening and require an answer.

1) *What is your immediate competition?* (Box A)
What do you know about the strengths and weaknesses of your competitors' strategies and resources? What are the trends in pricing contracts? Find out through your networks. How do you measure up to their price and quality? How will the balance between price and quality be specified and evaluated?

2) *What potential entrants are there?* (Box B)
Tho balanoo horo io to bo awaro of oxproooiono of intoroot, but not booomo overwhelmed by all that is researched. Examples in CCT have revealed considerable bluster, and the idea of HAG to developers may yet be another 'whimper' of change. But if there are expressions of interest, how would they set themselves up? How much would it cost? Can they buy expertise?

→

---

3) *What substitute services are available to your tenants?* (Box C)
Are there any real changes in substitute services? Is the 'right-to-buy' likely to bring major changes? Rents to mortgages and many other initiatives have been less successful. Are there local circumstances that will cause real shifts and affect your position?

4) *In what way are your tenants (buyers) becoming more influential?* (Box D)
Are the specific powers of tenants, acquired either through government legislation, local policy or community action, making changes which alter your competitive advantage? What are the views of your 'proxy buyers' – the politicians or committee members?

5) *In what ways are your suppliers changing their actions?* (Box E)
Are you aware of all the 'supplies' that you rely upon, and how these are changing? The government policies on housing are much discussed because its role as supplier has a major influence upon both local authorities and housing association organisations.

6) Draw up your responses to these questions and reach agreement as to *what are the critical changes and influences?*

7) *What should your organisation respond to?*
In other words, you begin to answer the question 'why must we change?' This can be usefully written up as an initial case for change. It will of course reveal much more; gaps in information, areas not thought about, but crucially, will lead you towards a working, competitive strategy.

## The challenge of comparison and pursuit of Best Value: benchmarking

A second way in which housing organisations, and increasingly many private and public organisations, are seeking to improve their effectiveness is to use some form of benchmarking to initiate change. It is not, contrary to some opinions just a method of analysis. It is both an analytic method and a process of investigating the differences of good practice in other organisations. As we have spelt it out here, it is something to be considered in its entirety, analysis and follow-through, before embarking on what is a change process. Nonetheless it is proving highly effective in clarifying where and how organisations should change.

The government is emphasising this type of process by imposing the duty on local authorities to pursue *Best Value* for all their services. Something similar could be extended to all bodies utilising public funds including housing associations. *Best Value* goes beyond the discipline of market mechanisms through CCT and requires continuous quality improvement as well. Benchmarking methods have a significant place in this approach.

The essence of the approach is to compare your organisation's performance and practices with those of others who are performing well. It is a management process which *searches* for best practices in the quality and costs of service delivery, *investigates* whether the practices elsewhere are transferable, and if so, seeks to *adapt* (rather than adopt) and implement them.

The principal benefits of benchmarking are that it enables (if the will is there) to:

- improve quality;
- lower costs;
- stimulate new ideas from outside and inside the organisation;
- challenge staff to review their practices and performance;
- provides a built-in process for continual improvement.

The benchmarking of any service involves four key stages. They are:

(1) *Agreeing the purpose of the benchmarking and the commitment to responding to its results.*
One local authority to which we were invited to assist with a benchmarking of its housing services took considerable time to establish the agreed scope and purpose. They wished to compare a range of their own service with good practice elsewhere on both quality and cost grounds. They also committed themselves to following through with appropriate changes. They recognised that it might involve changes at all levels, policy (affecting the committee directly), practice (affecting staff directly) and personnel (affecting both). Decisions would not be easy. Even in this first stage there needed to be careful communication, negotiation and fairness built into the process – something we discovered to our cost!

(2) *Searching for best practice and establishing a network of organisations interested in sharing data and good practice.*
Whilst it is possible to make comparisons on published and averaged data the process of benchmarking only really results in practical change if there is an openness to share information and practices with specific organisations, albeit within agreed confidentiality boundaries. In most cases there is an urgency that limits the search process for willing partners and narrows down those able to work to the time scale. At this stage there needs to be considerable effort in defining what services are to be covered, what *benchmarks* or measures are to be used and critically how these are to be defined.

In the local authority to which we have referred, we decided to cover some general statistics, e.g. units of stock, numbers of staff (and ratios of the two) and measures for the specific functions of voids, allocations, tenant participation, homelessness, development, sheltered housing and repairs. Within each we sought measures of service quality, volume and cost; three of the four core variables in any measure of service performance as set out in the performance model in Chapter 7, p.125. These three aspects we regard as the bare essentials.

Table 4.1 illustrates the measures for voids. Down the left hand side are the measures and across the top is the 'home' authority and the four other authorities in the network. The measures, which are by no means definitive, are:

- the non-lettable percentage of the stock and turnaround time in weeks – both regarded as quality measures (Q) albeit primarily oriented to the authority's interests in quality ;
- new relets per year – a volume measure (V);
- the cost of the service and numbers of staff (FTEs) – cost measures (C).

These provide partial coverage and measures of quality in particular and need treating with care. Nonetheless they provide a start for comparison.

**Table 4.1: Benchmarking of void management**

|  |  | Home | A | B | C | D |
|---|---|---|---|---|---|---|
| Non-lettable as % of stock | Q | 1.51% | 0.2% | 0.25% | 0.85% | 1.7% |
| Void turnaround time in weeks | Q | 6 | 2 | 1 | 4.45 | 6.5 |
| New relets p.a. Incl. national mobility | V | 191 | 361 | 223 | 431 | 446 |
| HM Staff costs | C | £23,954 | £57,107 |  | £25,300 |  |
| FTEs |  | 0.98 | 2 | 0.25 |  |  |

*(3) Comparison of data and initial investigation of differences.*
Once the data has been collected and agreed – no mean feat – then comparisons can be made. This will raise questions for investigation and not conclusions. It is clear from even a cursory glance at Table 4.1 that the 'home' authority needs to examine why it is not good on several measures and, in particular, why authority B is so good.

Differences that emerge can be the result of any one of four reasons. The precise reasons only become apparent upon detailed investigation. The four are:

- straight errors of fact;
- differences of detailed definition;
- differences of policy intention and activity;
- different ways of carrying out the activity.

It is the fourth reason that is the main focus of attention in benchmarking but organisations can learn much from investigating the others.

*(4) Learning from others and making changes.*
The powerful effect of benchmarking comes at this stage if it is to make a real difference. This typically involves the network of organisations meeting and agreeing what is to be followed up and who will take responsibility. It will often require the staff directly responsible for the function or process to make the visits, compare the processes and adapting experiences for use in their own organisation. This is the stage that is being followed through, at the time of writing, in our example above.

Major changes may be required at several levels; policy, practice and personnel, and these will need approval, but many significant changes can be made with small adaptations and learning by individuals. A phased approach is necessary to have a realistic implementation plan and to keep the momentum of the process going. One point that is crucial to remember; the process of comparison is not a once for all activity but must be utilised on a regular basis. *Best Value* has this process of continual improvement as a central tenet.

As we suggested at the beginning of this section, benchmarking is an analytic method and a organisational process rolled into one. It is therefore something to be considered in its entirety if it is to be used as a way of answering the question which began the chapter. In summary the elements of the method are set out below as an exercise for you to use.

---

### Exercise 4.3: The benchmarking stages

1) Reach agreement about the purpose, scope and commitment involved in the exercise.

2) Search for best practice and establish a network of organisations willing to share data within confidentiality limits and share practical details.

3) Compare and investigate differences.

4) Learn about the reasons for differences, implement changes and continue comparing.

---

## Evolutionary change: Stacey's model

Sometimes major change has to be evolutionary. It will not always be possible to develop a convincing strategy, however many 'Away Days' you hold. There can be a number of reasons for this:

- Your operating environment is turbulent and constantly changing.
- There are no clear ways forward.

- There are many planned and unplanned changes happening in the organisation.

For whatever of these reasons, or a combination of them, establishing a clear future direction may be, at this moment, difficult. Traditional views of strategic management would counsel against embarking upon change without having a clear picture of the future. This may, in today's turbulent environment, be a counsel of perfection. Slogans like 'costs must come down' or 'we must have a wider customer base' need a response.

There is mounting experience that this type of evolutionary change, with a rather vague start, may have to be embarked upon more often. The forces for change are so great they require a start to be made and the strategy and organisational response emerges as steps are taken. Ralph Stacey (1993) has suggested a model which helps cope with this uncertain process. He argues that the turbulence of the current operating environment for many organisations – he sometimes uses the word 'chaos' to describe it – requires an *open planning* approach. Before setting it out more formally an illustration of how it emerged in one housing organisation, may clarify the approach.

---

### Example 4.1: Evolutionary change in one housing department

This is well illustrated by one housing department we have worked with. It has had to develop its strategy in an evolutionary way, not by choice but by force of changing circumstances. Initially, in the early 1990s, conditions favoured a large stock voluntary transfer if the housing service was to improve and match emerging needs. Then, because of a mix of political and tenant reluctance, voluntary competitive tendering of the housing management (with the in-house team going to the winning contractor) became a more feasible goal. This, in turn, had to be altered when the authority changed political control and CCT, with support to an in-house bid, became the strategic goal. With the change of government the department has had to face both CCT in its death throes **and** *Best Value*.

On the surface this looks, and is, a repeated zigzag, with changes of direction. Underlying the process there has evolved a more subtle strategy for change, all within a broad objective of working for changes which improve the housing service in the community. Some of the key lessons which evolved from this sometimes painful experience, were:

- At any stage, even if a preferred option is clear, e.g. LSVT, then *alternative options*, e.g. VCT, CCT need to be worked out and updated as 'fall back' positions.
- Linked to this, the *key decision points* need time tabling – these may be tied to decisions to go ahead (or not) for the preferred option, e.g. LSVT, but also those for alternatives, e.g. lead times for CCT.

→

---

---

- *Regular review meetings* need to be established to examine progress, assess any changes to the desirability of the preferred option (i.e. its relative advantage to other options), and to revise management action and targets.
- *All preparatory work is assessed*, not just for its value in meeting the preferred option but how it might contribute as much as possible to the alternative options, e.g. establishing a team of change agents – a group of well respected, adaptable members of staff (other than line managers), who could communicate and lead practical changes – was established and has subsequently helped with all the changes.
- The handling of change, particularly changes in the strategic direction of change, requires an *adaptable organisation* which is both *supporting* of people in their emotions and the uncertainty *and demanding* of them in making specific changes.

---

Stacey makes the case for different types of planning to fit different circumstances. If your circumstances have many variables that are stable or are changing predictably, then conventional planning methods – he calls it *closed planning* – are appropriate. Typically this will involve knowing your goal clearly, project planning how to get there, regularly reviewing your progress against targets and eventually arriving, hopefully, at your predetermined goal. If many of the variables are not stable or predictable, then an open planning approach is more appropriate. Any organisation might need both methods for different areas of its activities; it is a 'horses for courses' approach.

To check which is appropriate to your situation his list of external and internal factors need considering (Table 4.2, on the next page). They will need choosing for relevance to the specific change you need to make. As a rough guide assign a weighting to each factor for the way in which it is likely to change: 1 for very small change through to 10 for major changes and 1 for predictable change up to 10 for totally unpredictable change. Add in any additional factors relevant to your organisation. Total each column and add the two together for a crude overall indication.

The maximum and minimum scores give the range. If the overall change you are wishing to make scores in the top third, then an open planning approach is appropriate, and if in the bottom third then a closed, i.e. project management approach is right. In the middle third, it may be worth starting with an open approach, and switching to a closed approach if the changes appear more certain as they are analysed.

If the key relevant factors are changing unpredictably and fast, then an open planning approach is necessary. Attempting to be precise in planning in such circumstances can be time consuming, create false certainty and lead to sudden lurches from one policy direction to another. Inevitably, the judgement will be subjective and the hope is that, eventually, open planning will lead to a closed planning.

---

**Table 4.2: Open or closed change – a checklist**

| Nature of change | Scale<br>small (1) to large (10) | Predictability<br>high (1) to low (10) |
|---|---|---|
| External factors: | | |
| • Customer requirements | | |
| • Government regulations | | |
| • Competitor behaviour | | |
| • Cost and quality structures<br>  in the industry | | |
| • Technology use and changes | | |
| • Trading condition | | |
| | | |
| Internal factors: | | |
| • Policy and political situation | | |
| • Organisation's ability to deliver | | |
| • Work processes and systems | | |
| • Service improvement | | |
| • Staff motivation | | |
| • Quality of staff | | |
| • Priorities and the management<br>  of them | | |
| | | |
| Totals | | |

Based on the Stacey model of open planning, how do you start? Stacey suggests a number of stages not unlike those that evolved in the housing department example outlined earlier. The key elements are:

*Be as clear as possible about what change is required of you*, e.g. to drastically improve customer responsiveness, reduce costs by 20 per cent, shift your range of services to a more secure base. The end product might not be clear but the broad direction might be. Figure 4.3 sets this out diagrammatically. At your current position A, you have only an outline view of where to go, i.e. B1.

**Figure 4.3: Open planning**

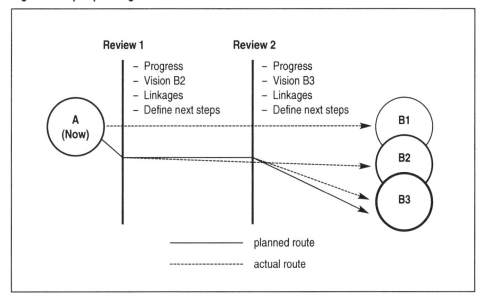

Starting off in the broad direction you have set (B1) will require the *generation of ideas*, e.g. how to reduce costs; *the collection of data*, e.g. what are typical benchmark costs in the social housing sector? What are internal costs?

*Establish regular review points* (review 1, 2, Figure 4.3). These are crucial to this approach. Unlike most project planning which has review points to assess progress and get back (if necessary) on target, these review points do four things:

- Review progress and findings (solid line in Figure 4.3).
- Assess whether B1 is the right goal and perhaps revise it to a new goal B2, e.g. cutting costs by 20 per cent may be impractical and 15 per cent cuts, plus generating income, may be more feasible.
- Assess the linkages between new goals and the organisation's ongoing activities – are there connections/synergies?
- Define the next stages of work.

*Continue reviewing* (review 2) and re-directing the work (goal B3) until enough clarity emerges to consider the goal fixed and the work can be project planned.

Whilst this model of assessing and managing major change is not wholly new, it is only now that it is gaining acceptability. Having taken many years for our housing organisations to accept the vision setting approach, i.e. think strategically, set clear targets and project manage the change, it can seem like a relaxation of a discipline that has been hard won. We would argue it is not either/or, rather, that in uncertain circumstances one must start *open* before using the very useful disciplines of *closed* planning, as your future direction becomes more coherent and clear. Many private and public organisations are finding this 'horses for course' approach a necessity rather than a luxury.

## Intractable internal problems: Ohmae's technique

The three techniques we have just outlined deal with housing organisations responding to external pressures for change; competition, comparison and the other more general pressures. Whilst most significant changes in our organisations ought to be responding to external pressures – we would reiterate Ansoff's point that for organisations to survive they must be *environmentally driven* – there are occasions when internal problems may be critical.

Some organisational problems start and finish with management adopting the familiar problem-solving methods. Often this involves clearly identifying the problem and looking for solutions which have worked in the past, e.g. the maintenance budget is forecast to overspend (again) and so a method of dealing only with priority work is imposed. Yet there are some internal, organisational problems which require a more rigorous analysis and resolution. Typically these are:

- Problems which have failed to be solved by familiar methods, e.g. repeatedly underspending or overspending budgets.
- Problems which, if allowed to continue, will significantly affect the effectiveness, or even threaten the credibility or survival, of the organisation, e.g. heavy staff turnover through very poor morale, and rapidly escalating costs.

Kenichi Ohmae, author of the well regarded book *The Mind of the Strategist* (1983), set out a technique which helps deal with such problems in a strategic way. It is a technique which, above all else, helps you develop the right questions which can then be answered appropriately.

By way of illustration, he cites a business whose overtime payments are becoming so high they begin to threaten the competitive position of the company's product. The *obvious* question is, therefore, how to control and reduce overtime payments. If this is the question, the answers may be to 'work harder during regular hours'; 'have shorter lunch breaks'; or 'forbid private telephone calls'. Yet this, Ohmae argues, is just to remedy the symptoms for this organisation. The wider question is how to increase productive capacity within acceptable costs – in other words to ask a question framed for a longer term solution. Based on his consultancy the company went to work at casting their *analytic nets* much wider and, as a result caught bigger *fish of solutions*, more suitable to the longer run resolution of the problem.

The technique he adopts is a stage-by-stage process, set out in an adapted form in Figure 4.4. Normally we identify the problem and 'concrete' evidence of it, and take the typical short circuit to solutions and draft action plans. This, let us reiterate, may be quite appropriate for many, if not most, internal problems. If, however, a thorough analysis is needed, then Ohmae suggests an initial four stages for *solving the problem*:

(1) *Defining the concrete evidence:* What is the actual evidence that a problem exists?

(2) *Grouping by topic or theme:* What goes with what? What topics or themes are emerging?

(3) *Abstracting the underlying issues:* What are the precise issues giving rise to the different topics or themes?

(4) *Determining possible approaches:* What appropriate types of approaches or options are there to these issues? (A typical mistake is to resolve problems of one kind – e.g. attitudes and systems – by solutions of another – e.g. restructuring).

**Figure 4.4: Stages of strategic thinking**

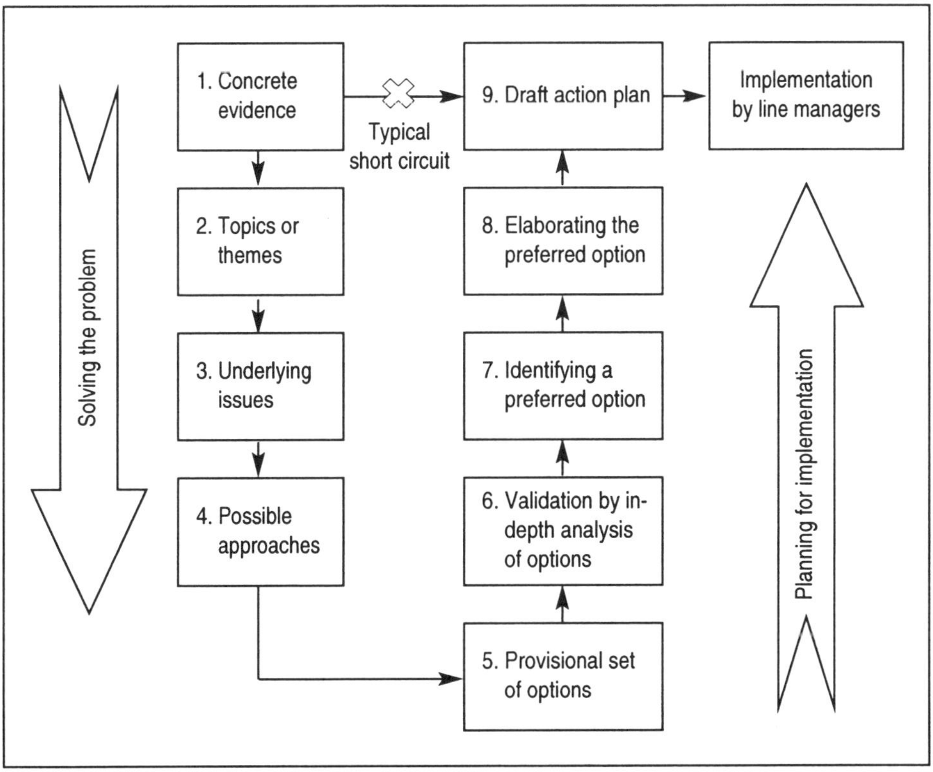

(Adapted from *The Mind of the Strategist*)

This, he follows with five stages of *'planning for implementation'*, which are more familiar:

(5) *Formulating options:* What range of solutions can you generate?

(6) *Validating by in-depth analysis:* What further analysis and information is necessary to identify the strengths and weaknesses of the options?

(7) *Identifying a preferred option:* Is there one option that is a front runner? Can it incorporate the strengths of other options?

(8) *Elaborating the preferred option:* What practical shape would the preferred option take?

(9) *Drafting an action plan:* What form of action plan would provide a practical way of implementing the chosen option or solution?

One housing association manager chose to use this technique to deal with an emerging problem in hostel housing for which he was responsible. Not unlike Ohmae's example, his association was faced with mounting staff costs, primarily arising from heavy overtime payments to cover sickness, vacancies and additional workload. As an association providing a hostel service, they were feeling the increased pressures on community care budgets and the additional costs began to make them uncompetitive. Rather than going in for a heavy cost controlling exercise, he decided to assess the problem more widely using Ohmae's model.

Table 4.3 sets out the first four initial *stages of problem-solving* which were the more unusual and difficult for the manager. We have left off the more familiar later stages of *planning for the implementation* which he is currently working through. Briefly, he found the following:

- *Defining the concrete evidence.* This evidence, when collected, raised a much wider set of concerns e.g. column (1), yet greater focus in some respects, e.g. particular hostels were critical.
- *Grouping by topic or theme.* Rather than just a series of cost control themes, there were three overlapping ones – personnel, finance and strategic. Not only was there a personnel theme, covering many familiar areas including personal practices in particular hostels and agreements; financial themes of cost control and rent levels; but also strategic issues of trends in care costs, deficit costing and their place as a provider.
- *Abstracting the underlying issues.* This stage forced a narrowing down of the same key underlying issues – the 'lack of clarity' about personnel policing and practices, the 'high costs' and 'lack of clear agreement' about their financial basis, and 'fixed ideas about staff cover' which will affect the strategic future of the service.

- *Determining possible approaches.* At this stage a wide range of approaches began to emerge, from the more obvious one of setting up clear policies on overtime and sickness, to establishing strategic initiatives on staffing budgets and longer term funding of care costs.

**Table 4.3: Analysis of a problem of staff costs**

| 1) Concrete evidence | 2) Topic or theme | 3) Underlying issues | 4) Positive approaches |
|---|---|---|---|
| Particular hostels with high staff vacancies and sickness absence | | Lack of clarity | Set up policy on overtime and sickness |
| Extensive use of part time staff | ⌐ Personnel | Fixed ideas on staff cover | Evaluate cost of part/ full time staff |
| Difficulty of meeting the need for 24 hour cover | | | Review staffing policy |
| | | | |
| Cumulative effects of the factors above on care costs | | | Review to include staff and managers |
| Ad hoc arrangements for pay | ⌐ Finance | High cost and no clear agreement | Budgets with clear agreements |
| Extensive deficit costs | | | Funding for care costs |

The manager concerned is pleased with this wider analysis of his problems and whilst the technique does widen the problem, and seemingly make it more intractable before narrowing it down, it does attempt to tackle the roots of problems and provide a longer term solution. Typically, it slows down over-speedy management thinking of 'problem straight into solution' and draws others into the process to test and widen both the analysis and resolutions. It's not for all problems, only the major or intractable.

# Support for the change

This section may appear odd in a chapter about *why must we change?* If, however, the initial assessment of the question does not include some views (or likely views) by interested and influential parties, the change may be short lived. Here we suggest you make use of a stakeholder analysis. For it to have its full usefulness, it needs to be a continuing activity in the implementation process, and we make some suggestions at the end of the section for use at later stages.

Stakeholder analysis has had an increasing usefulness in the management of change and an increasing profile in the national political sphere (with the new government's promotion of the stakeholder society). It seeks to identify the various parties with a 'stake' or interest in the change. The most common variant is one which suggests six types of stakeholding (Handy):

- The *customers'* interests, who purchase goods and services. This needs extending to those who take part in expressing the interests of the customers of social housing, namely tenants' groups, interest groups (e.g. Shelter, TPAS), the local council housing committee, the housing association committee and the government, through legislative measures.
- The *financier and/or shareholder*, who may have money invested. This extends to local council finance, Housing Corporation finance and overall financial regime of the government regarding social housing.
- The *suppliers'* interests, who provide any type of input necessary for the business to function (parallels with Porter's 'Five Box' Model are clear with this interest).
- The *employees'* interests, who have a range of experiences and expectations, and in some cases trade union representation.
- The local *community*, who have an interest in the business as an employer, buyer, and possibly producer of environmental impacts such as traffic and pollution.
- The *societal* interests, expressed through political views and actions, formal and informal, and through media approval and disapproval.

These six do represent a good starting point, even if they need to be substantially elaborated and made relevant to your organisation. An outline of an initial stakeholder analysis is set out below. This will need applying to the specific change you wish to make. It is stakeholders' views of your change that are important, not necessarily what they think of your organisation overall.

## Exercise 4.4: Initial stakeholder analysis

Your management team needs to work through the following stages:

1) Identifying the specific stakeholders in the situation. Who has an ability to influence what and *how* things happen? A flip chart with a 'wheel' diagram can be particularly helpful, as shown below. Your committee (whether housing association or local authority) will need separate identification, because they will have different views from you. Other groupings will need subdividing as appropriate.

2) Identify what are their interests in making (or not making) a change. It may be necessary to separate *what they want to get away from* (the push for change) from *what they want*. At this early stage, you may be second guessing about what they think.

3) Take an overall look at the picture, and in particular ask yourself:

- Who is seeking *change from* the present situation?
- What *weight* should this be given to particular views and how are their *interests served*?
- What are their likely ideas about what to *change to*?

4) Draw your initial conclusions together. Is your internal management team's view about change diminished or enhanced?

Stakeholder analysis goes well beyond the stage we have taken it to here and the subject of this chapter. It is something that is worth continuing to run throughout any change process (p.152). The following may be appropriate next steps:

- Have *direct discussions* with those with stakes or interests. Clearly, issues of sensitivity and care over setting 'hares running' need to shape the process. However, direct evidence will enhance the analysis under stage 2 above.
- Use the information about *what alternatives* they may want to develop as *options for change* (in addition to those you are generating; see next chapter).
- Check whether there are strong views about *how change* might happen.

At this stage, you would perhaps be drawing the views and options together. Beyond this stage it is important to use the stakeholders' analyses to periodically identify any shifts in demands and to negotiate modifications as you proceed with the overall change. This will involve:

- Drawing up a clear programme of *who, in what order, and when* to discuss the plans. Be clear what is open to negotiation and what is for information.
- Where there are problems and differences, establish *how far you are to negotiate.*
- Use the programme to *build support and consensus* where possible, and address how you might deal with resistance to change.
- Consider whether a *regular review session* with stakeholders is desirable to keep them on board and negotiate the implementation as it happens.

## Conclusion: why must we change? – your answers

This chapter has argued that a clear, convincing and committed answer is necessary to the question of 'why must we change?' We have suggested that you:

- Assess your starting point – the *triggers* for change.
- Analyse the situation – four *techniques* have been outlined.
- Clarify the *commitment* to change – perhaps undertaking the first stages of a stakeholder analysis.

The results of this should provide answers. It is only active debate, challenge and reworking that will give you clarity, conviction and commitment to the changes. This will take time but appropriate pacing is critical. Taking too much time and you may be charged with indecisiveness, taking too little and you may suffer a credibility problem – 'it was dreamed up in the bath'!

Answering the question *'why must we change?'* inevitably generates ideas, analysis and views about *'where are we going?'* – the subject of Chapter 6 and at some point this should be incorporated there.

## Further reading

Ansoff, I. (1987) (Chapter 19) *Corporate Strategy*, Penguin, London.

Bogan, C.E. and English, M.J. (1994) (Chapters 3,4,5) *Benchmarking for Best Practice*, McGraw-Hill, New York.

Handy, C. (1994) (Chapter 8) *The Empty Raincoat*, Hutchinson, London.

Moore, J.I. (1992) (Chapter 4 on Michael Porter) *Writers on Strategy and Strategic Management*, Penguin, London.

Ohmae, K. (1983) *The Mind of the Strategist*, Penguin, London.

Stacey, R. (1993) (Chapter 8) *Strategic Management and Organisational Dynamics*, Pitman, London.

# CHAPTER 5:
# Where are we now?

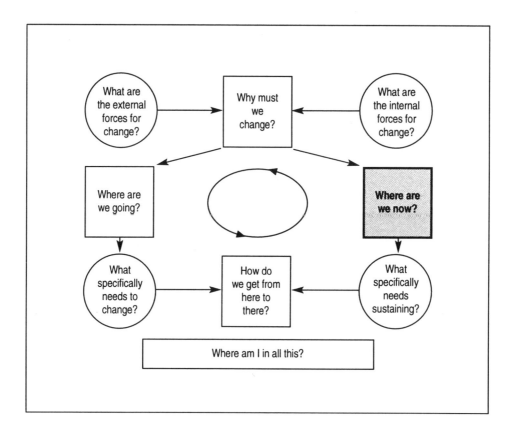

**Objectives**
After reading this chapter you should be able to:

- understand the purpose and content of a capability assessment;
- appreciate the importance of organisational culture and values;
- conduct the analysis and writing of a capability assessment;
- identify the possible changes which might be made to your organisation.

# Introduction

Chapter 4 posed some questions about why your organisation must change. The purpose of this chapter is to examine how you might assess the present position of your housing organisation through a **capability assessment** and to assist senior managers to undertake such a review. It is now necessary to establish why such an assessment is required.

Bowman and Asch (1987) argue that,

> *"the assessment of the internal position is of some importance in evaluating the enterprise's capabilities in the light of its resources."*

Put simply, if managers and committee members are to plan the development of their organisation (how to get to a certain point), then it is important to know where you are starting from. Beckhard and Harris (1987) also point out that organisational managers often make incorrect assumptions about the current state (capability) of their organisation when they are developing change strategies. If this happens then subsequent action or implementation plans may become confused, organisations may encounter unexpected resistance and probably fail to achieve the desired change (pp.57-58). As a rule of thumb, the more information gathered, the more accurate the assessment of the present position is likely to be and the insights gathered will be of a multi-dimensional nature – cross cutting investigations which review all aspects of, and strata within, your organisation.

The preparation of a capability assessment will assist with the management of change since organisations should only change what needs 'fixing' rather than every aspect of the organisation. This also applies to development needs of individuals – you need only provide training and development assistance for those who need it!

But there are obviously resource and time limits to data collection and this chapter focuses on helping senior housing managers to decide how much, and in what detail, information is required to present an accurate picture of the condition of your housing organisation. With respect to judging the amount of work which housing organisations wish to undertake, Fitzgeorge-Butler (1997) provides an in-depth analysis of how to carry out a capability assessment for Best Value and contrasts two types:

- An overview – a sketch review.
- A fundamental review – an in-depth study.

# Components of an overview

This can be broadly expressed as an investigation into the *'where are we now?'* question. The following is provided as an illustrative procedure, namely:

- Setting out the present purposes, aims and objectives of all service areas, especially policy priorities.
- Assess fit or match with present customer requirements.
- Effectiveness in meeting present objectives etc. (service user group feedback).
- Utilisation of national comparator and local information (PIs; audit reports; last review etc.).
- How effective is the council likely to be in the future with its present mix of competencies and capabilities?

## Components of a fundamental review

A fundamental review, as suggested by the term, is a more in-depth analysis of the organisation, incorporating the following illustrative aspects:

- Overview to provide pointers for investigation (the first tranche of analysis).
- Customer needs analysis.
- Quality audits.
- Service profile.
- Cultural analysis.

Grundy (1993) situates his capability analysis (assessment) in a direct relationship with the need to analyse the competition and the external environment in order to make plans to reach the strategic vision stage (p.119). He also provides some useful checklists in order to determine organisation capability (pp.114-117).

But when considering drawing up a capability assessment, or diagnosing what needs to change, it is inevitable that we shall have in our minds some concept of the organisation as a 'system'. Warner Burke (1982) has characterised this as an 'open system'. The inputs (information and material in whatever form) which come into it, are transformed, and exit as outputs (as goods or services for customers) (p.64). So what we are actually analysing here is the effectiveness with which the organisation handles this process, section by section, team by team, and function by function.

The concept of preparing a capability assessment may be comparatively new to many housing managers but it is necessary for two principal reasons. Firstly, it is used in the strategic planning context to identify the precise areas for which implementation plans must be made in order to effectively deliver a corporate or business plan and to take an overall strategic view of the process. Even more importantly, it will identify, as already mentioned, the precise areas in which change is required, and what must be addressed and managed in a change process.

The organisation of this chapter reflects, and is ordered around, the contents of the capability assessment itself. It is necessary to explain in greater detail the meanings of some of the terms and concepts used in this discussion, especially questions identifying core values and their usage and about the analysis and interpretation of organisational cultural data. This allows managers to engage in some prior analysis to ensure that the construction of a capability assessment is understood, and put into an organisational context.

This chapter provides senior managers with the underlying concepts and ideas to understand the process *and* a set of tools with which to produce an accurate and useful analysis.

Finally, it is difficult to conceive of housing managers planning to undergo large-scale change without preparing a capability assessment and without knowing where the difficulties, problems and obstacles lie within the existing organisation and with its implementation. It is, however, recognised that this will be a challenging process for many organisations, and even threatening for some, but is important for managers to face up to the reality of how things *are* done within their housing organisation. But, perhaps paradoxically, senior managers will gain much support *and* credit for encouraging such a process, seeing it through and most crucially of all, acting upon the information.

## Why carry out a capability assessment?

There are some important reasons why senior managers should instigate such a review (and it is of special importance when preparing for Best Value (Fitzgeorge-Butler, 1997), namely to:

- provide crucial up-to-date information about the efficiency, effectiveness and economy of present service provision;
- identify past issues/difficulties which continue to influence the organisation – a short history;
- cost the provision of existing services *by activity* (activity costing);
- assess the effectiveness of existing policies, procedures, and practices by means of a review (what works, what doesn't, what needs improving, what doesn't);
- assess the competence and capabilities of managers and staff *at all levels*;
- discover the perceptions of stakeholders, partners and customers about the existing service provision (What do they think needs changing? What could make partnership more effective?);

- discover possible obstacles/barriers facing the organisation as it manages change *and* proposals on how these might be overcome;
- provide evidence on which proposals for improvements, changes, and new methods of working can be based. Such changes may be agreed in co-operation and collaboration with all stakeholders *and* in the light of the proposed values and vision of the organisation (What strategic and operational changes are suggested by the medium term organisational goals?).

Hofer and Schendel (1978) summarise the process by identifying three stages for drawing up a capability assessment:

(1) The development of a profile of principal skills and resources.
(2) A comparison of this resource profile with the services being offered and market requirements in order to identify organisational strengths and weaknesses.
(3) Strengths and weaknesses compared with major competitors to identify areas where significant competitive advantage exists (p.145).

But it must always be remembered that this is a dynamic and multi-dimensional process in which managers are attempting to learn from past success or failure.

## Components of the capability assessment

There are various aspects to establishing **where we are now** but they revolve around comparing three key areas:

- actual achievement against stated or official objectives;
- the relative success in implementing stated strategies; and
- the expectations and aspirations of stakeholders.

(Thompson, 1997, p.177)

The last point reinforces the emphasis placed at the end of Chapter 4 on the importance of stakeholders' views. However, such comparisons, as suggested above, will also begin to uncover the issues, obstacles and difficulties which the organisation is encountering as it attempts to meet its aims and objectives. It is important to bear in mind how housing organisations tend to work. This will also enable your organisation to make connections between an analysis of your present position and the perceived understanding of how your housing organisation operates.

The first objective, however, is to explain two key concepts, 'organisational culture' and 'values', which will have an important impact on the main capability assessment.

# What is organisational culture?

The literature explains 'organisational culture' by referring to a number of elements with which it is composed. We have already looked at it briefly in Chapter 3. One way of defining culture is to express it simply in terms of 'the way things are done' in our organisation. This simple definition does not tell us much about the term culture but it does signify the all embracing nature of the concept.

In more detail, the specific elements or components of organisational culture can be summarised, as follows:

- how people describe their organisation;
- the total pattern of managerial and staff behaviour within the organisation;
- the rules which guide and condition behaviour within a housing organisation;
- descriptions about human relationships within the organisation;
- the ideology which lies behind organisational culture;
- the history of the organisation;
- the ways in which behaviour is transmitted within organisations;
- the taken-for-granted nature of culture;
- the constantly changing or dynamic of organisational cultures;
- the importance of the language used within organisations;
- the existence of both overt and covert cultures;
- the possibility of mismatches between the organisational culture which managers want and the actual culture – a case of people saying one thing and doing another.

Additionally, Jackson and Palmer (1989) point out that in not-for-profit organisations, such as housing, performance can be measured more effectively by taking into account cultural and change issues (the underlying factors to internal change, see Chapter 3, pp.26-31). Specifically, the climate must be right, with managers thinking clearly about what activities should be measured and what the objectives of these activities are. It is also important to ask users how effective they perceive such organisations to be.

# The importance of values

One of the controlling factors within organisations is their explicit or implicit values. All organisations have values whether they are clearly stated or not. It must be recognised that paid staff have personal values which inevitably affect and colour the way they approach their work. These values, both personal and organisational, need to be carefully explored in order to identify those values which work against the purposes of a given organisation. For example, some managers and staff may hold racist or sexist views. But most housing organisations now have strongly worded equal opportunity statements and policies. The key is to root out discriminatory beliefs and attitudes at work by monitoring the effect of anti-discriminatory policies. This is a good example of a possible mismatch between what an organisation says it does and what it actually does.

It is not easy to alter such dysfunctional attitudes but the very least that can be expected is that when such staff are at work they must follow the agreed values of the organisation. It is therefore of considerable importance that organisational values are explicit and clearly stated, that conflicts between personal and organisational values are explored and that an organisation 'enforces' their stated values at all levels.

The real meaning of organisational values need to be closely examined so that they can be more effectively put into operation and 'owned' by all organisational members. This is neither an easy nor comfortable process but is the only way that organisational cultures can be made 'fit for their purpose' within housing agencies.

The reason for this is that values are also a major factor in determining both organisational cultures and the personal behaviour of managers and staff. It must also be remembered that the identification of core values *must come before* a desired culture can be planned for, and introduced. The root cause of many of the difficulties faced by organisations is the lack of attention being paid to the encouragement of positive values.

## Difficulties and obstacles facing housing organisations

Before moving on to explaining the process of preparing a capability assessment, it is useful to briefly explore the ways in which obstacles and difficulties with respect to the implementation of change might become apparent. What are the common ones facing housing organisations?

These might be:

- expectations too high or unrealistic;
- lack of organisational ability to complete tasks;
- management ineffectiveness;
- staff lacking in skills, knowledge or capabilities;
- prior changes mismanaged;
- an inappropriate management style;
- managers not supporting their staff;
- organisation demoralised (i.e. constant change, poor management);

- managers and staff do not know the aims and objectives of the organisation;
- lack of priority given to key issues;
- ineffective teamworking;
- lack of training and development for managers and staff;
- managers and staff not involved in decision-making;
- poor communication up and down the organisation;
- a lack of personal commitment and responsibility.

From this list it can be seen that it might be useful to engage in some preliminary organisational analysis to reveal such difficulties *before* the change process begins, or at the very least, before plans are made to overcome them during the process. Fundamentally, it may not even be possible for change to occur if, for example, poor communication persists. Effective communication is a prior requirement for successful change processes. Difficulties and obstacles will rapidly become apparent during the process of drawing up a capability assessment and a separate statement should be made about them *and* urgently addressed by senior managers.

We suggest a preliminary mapping exercise in order to identify clusters of change problems. Indeed this kind of approach is suggested by the 'overview' required for Best Value pilot authorities.

The illustrations above have resulted in long lists of individual change issues and it is therefore more useful to think about clusters of issues, say those issues linked to poor communication or the development of competencies and skills within your organisation. The descriptions should specify three factors: **who** (groups of individuals where problems exist), **what** (the organisational processes associated problems and issues) and **how** (the consequences for the organisation of perceived difficulties). You will then be able to spot key issues or root causes of current organisational weaknesses. Unfortunately, this can turn into a somewhat negative exercise, which might be tempered and offset through undertaking the same exercise concentrating on the strengths of your housing organisation. The above exercise will help when it comes to deciding what to change and what transitional arrangements are required for sustaining the present business whilst changes are made (see Chapter 6).

## Methods of analysis

Perhaps the most important factor in conducting a review of housing organisations is the methods of analysis used to assess their strengths, weaknesses, opportunities and the perceived threats facing them. This is usually undertaken by means of a SWOT analysis, but aspects of this type of investigation can also be included in an organisational survey (as indicated below) and has also been partially used for understanding the external and internal forces for change (Chapter 3, p.31).

There are, however other methods by which this kind of analysis can be undertaken and these will be briefly explained. Although this is the beginning of the business planning and strategic planning process, it is also necessary to assess the current performance of the organisation and there are various methods by which this can be achieved.

It is also useful to appraise and evaluate the present culture of housing organisations, which is achieved principally by adopting a survey methodology, which can either be undertaken by using a sample survey or by use of a semi-structured questionnaire which allows the researcher to ask follow-up questions. This allows the collection of more anecdotal information about culture, which tends to pin-point the areas of particular difficulty. When this process is completed it will then be necessary to establish, drawing from the cultural and all the other findings, the need for change which connects with the need to achieve the agreed vision and overall aims of the organisation. On the other hand, there will be aspects of the organisational culture and present functioning which managers will be anxious to retain since they perform well and fit in with the desired changes. This process of identifying what to change can probably be best thought of in terms of comparing the current state of your organisation with its functioning under ideal conditions. Preparing the ideal culture is, however, inextricably linked with the vision for your housing organisation and its values or guiding principles.

The following are the most usual methods of analysis:

1. The starting point: existing information.
2. SWOT analysis.
3. Picturing the organisation (pictorial representation of organisational issues).
4. Organisation and cultural surveys (through formal questionnaires to managers, staff, customers and stakeholders).
   (a) Organisational surveys.
   (b) Cultural surveys.
   (c) Managers surveys.
   (d) Staff surveys.
   (e) Other stakeholder surveys.
   (f) Customer surveys.
   (g) Time log surveys.
   (h) Service demand surveys.
   (i) Analysis of surveys.
5. Diagnostic interviews (informal but probing with only a minimum of structure).
6. Personal observation.
7. Identification of training needs.
8. Information from training courses.
9. Discussion groups (sometimes called 'focus' or 'sensing' groups) (SWOT analysis is a variant of this).

10. Content analysis of documents and published material.
11. Managerial experiences on the front linc.

We shall now consider each of these methods in turn.

# Preparing a capability assessment – the process

This information is provided in some detail so that the extent and range of the relevant activities can be studied in-depth by managers (additional and supporting information is provided later under these headings).

It is also suggested that stages 1, 2 and 4b might also be useful for the 'overview' (Best Value) process – a much shortened version of the capability assessment. However, care must be exercised since it is clear that with less information collected, the 'fix' on what needs to change will also be less accurate.

## 1. The starting point: existing information

This stage involves the collection of existing information about the functioning of the housing organisation. The following activities should be undertaken:

- Collect information about organisational aims/objectives – the strategic orientation of the organisation.
- Map (list) all services *currently* provided and all activities associated with them.

This process will suggest some further key questions and activities such as:

What services are currently provided?
List of *all* activities
For whom?
By whom?
How are they currently provided?
To what standard?
With what resources?
At what cost (using current labour/overhead costing formulas)?
How much of this information *currently* exists – recent reviews, management information systems data, training needs analyses, IIP audits etc.?

It will therefore be necessary to collect all the available and current information such as the following: policy statements; procedure manuals (or equivalent); cost information; results of mapping exercise (lists of services/activities); quantitative information about customer categories (specific services provided for specific customers); reports/audits on or about the organisation; and the volume of work/usage of existing services?

This analysis must always be undertaken since it provides the basic information, and starting point for the different analytical techniques explained below.

## 2. SWOT analysis

We have already mentioned SWOT analysis in Chapter 3 in connection with identifying the internal forces for change. It is an important method of analysis and must be considered essential to the process. The technique is mentioned in most textbooks and refers, as the mnemonic infers, to four organisational aspects,

> Strengths
> Weaknesses
> Opportunities
> Threats

The idea is that groups of managers and staff can brainstorm each factor in turn to determine what they consider to be the key elements under each factor.

For example, one group may feel that in respect of strengths they are strong in the following areas:

> Teamwork
> Commitment
> Understanding organisational objectives

but are weak in terms of

> Communication
> Strategic (forward) planning
> Getting results on time

Beckhard and Harris (1987) have suggested an alternative way of looking at this question by listing individuals and groups who are critical to the change effort with rankings (high, medium, and low) as to their readiness and capability for change (p.63). This simple method, although somewhat rough and ready, can help focus attention on the areas which must be worked on (weaknesses) to create the critical energy needed for change to occur.

But another important aspect of the analysis is the roles managers play at different levels within the organisation – strategic or operational. This also relates back to the model for strategic planning and management – what senior managers ought to be doing (planning and managing strategically).

SWOT analysis should also provide sufficient information to provide anecdotal information as to the weaknesses of particular organisational units (see Chapter 3, p.31-32 for a worked example).

## 3. Picturing the organisation

This uses a method of pictorial analysis for looking at the culture of the organisation. We have found that managers greatly enjoy completing it!

The method is relatively simple:

- Supply your managers with a piece of flip-chart paper and appropriate pen.
- Ask them to draw a representation of how they perceive the organisation.
- On completion, ask them to explain their drawing.

Their interpretations will be wide-ranging. We have seen pictures depicting their part of the organisation isolated from the remainder of the organisation (say, on a island distanced from the rest), poor communication, dominant figures within the management team and the organisation (towering figures dwarfing the rest), power cultures (dominant figures gesticulating to others) and so forth. **The important point, however, is to get those who draw the pictures to interpret them to the rest of the group.** This method can provide some valuable insights into the functioning and culture of the organisation but is not considered essential to the process.

## 4. Organisational and cultural surveys

Surveys are an important tool for collecting information in a more formal way about the overall functioning of your housing organisation. Some kind of survey of stakeholders, managers and staff must be carried out.

### a) Organisational surveys
There are a number of key factors in organisational surveys. Firstly, the phrasing questions is important, since like a SWOT analysis, it can provide a snapshot of the challenges, difficulties and issues currently facing the organisation. Secondly, it is useful to have such questions answered as objectively as possible and, finally, managers and staff must have confidence both in the results themselves and the interpretation of them. The following list sets out some of the commonly asked key general questions and could be completed as an exercise.

---

### Exercise 5.1: Key questions for your organisation

1. What are the current issues and problems facing your organisation?

2. How do you feel about working within this organisation?

3. What are the strengths of this organisation?

4. What are its weaker points?

5. Does the organisation structure deliver achievement or help you meet aims and objectives? If not, why not?

6. Do your operating systems enable you to deliver the above? If not, why not?

7. Do you have strategies which help you to deliver the above?

8. What is the culture of your housing organisation?

---

Remember that your observations and thoughts will be anecdotal at this stage and will need to be tested out with other organisational members. Indeed perceptions, may vary from division to division and team to team.

It is also possible to address a questionnaire more specifically to the question of the current state of the organisation and the following is a list of a number of further key questions which address these issues.

---

### Questionnaire 5.1: The culture of the organisation

1. Are organisational aims and objectives widely known and shared throughout the organisation and is managerial and staff energy consistently directed towards achieving them?

2. Do people feel free to raise actual or potential difficulties and problems because they know they will be addressed?

3. Will managers and staff work collaboratively together to solve problems?

4. Is non-conforming behaviour tolerated within the organisation?

5. Is decision-making determined by ability, sense of personal responsibility, availability of information and workload rather than controlled by top managers?

→

---

6. Does teamwork play a noticeable part in planning, setting standards and discipline?

7. Are people lower down in the organisation both valued and respected?

8. Are feelings, personal needs and human relationships tackled by teams on a regular basis?

9. Is collaboration freely entered into by all managers and staff – help is requested and freely given?

10. Do teams compete but in a spirit of achieving agreed objectives and targets?

11. In a crisis, do people work together until it is solved?

12. Are conflicts dealt with openly with people saying what they want and others expected to do the same?

13. Is there a lot of on-the-job learning within your organisation, based on a willingness to give, seek and use feedback and advice?

14. Is progress towards agreed objectives and targets jointly and regularly reviewed by teams at all levels?

15. Are relationships honest with people caring about each other, without undercurrents of fear?

16. Are people excited and optimistic about coming to work?

17. Do managers exercise flexible leadership according to situations?

18. Is there a high degree of trust and feeling of mutual responsibility between people within your organisation?

19. Do people generally know what is and is not important to the organisation?

Managers will probably notice that there are a number of underlying values in the above list of questions such as, high personal responsibility and involvement, openness, collaboration, co-operation, management through influence not control, teamwork, self-discipline, respect for others, a bias to learning together, honesty in relationships, people are 'turned on' and trust. A most important point is that if such values are widely disseminated and acted upon within your organisation it will be 'healthy' and highly effective.

It is also clear that such surveys can also produce valuable information about important subjects such as:

- the values of managers and staff;
- assumptions about the world and customers brought to the workplace by managers and staff;
- the effectiveness of senior and middle managers;
- the types of management and leadership styles in use;
- whether information is communicated effectively up and down the organisation;
- the effect of the size of an organisation on its functioning and effectiveness;
- how do committees and senior managers monitor the achievement of specific objectives;
- systems of accountability – both for tasks undertaken and the behaviour of managers and staff;
- the allocation of human, financial and human resources.

### b) Cultural surveys

Although there is considerable overlap between organisational and cultural surveys, it is worth drawing your attention to the idea of the 'cultural web' which is set out in Faulkner and Johnson (1992). This links together a number of factors – stories and myths; rituals and routines; control systems; organisational structures, power structures and other organisational symbols – and may be used as a convenient device for audit use, especially with managers.

Broadly, cultural surveys address the ways in which the values of your organisation are translated into practice in terms of the behaviour of managers and staff. Values define organisational culture.

Exercises, used in a group, will access values in action and provide information about the features of the existing organisational culture. Given the overlap between surveys targeted at specific people and cultural surveys, it is often possible to draw inferences from the former about the organisational culture. If the cultural patterns are unclear further analysis should be attempted. The focus is always upon identifying what needs to change and one must continue to analyse the organisation until this is accomplished.

It is important that managers now make some preliminary attempt to analyse what the above elements might mean to their organisation and to find some examples to illustrate those meanings.

It will not matter if at this stage your ideas are only generalised or sketchy. The important task is to discuss your ideas and thoughts about the culture of your organisation and to try to make sense of them. It is much easier to attempt this outline analysis within a team or group perhaps as a team exercise.

Some possible negative aspects of culture which may appear in your lists are provided for illustrative purposes (in no particular order):

| | |
|---|---|
| Survival/crisis management | Life hectic/chaotic |
| Stress/pressure ignored | Preoccupation with 'what' not 'how' |
| Nothing really changes | Avoidance of 'real' issues |
| Decentralisation exported 'red tape' | Unhelpful to the public |
| Under-utilisation of staff skills | Submerged by change |
| Change poorly understood | Lack of direction/purpose |
| Inadequate resources | Judging customers |
| Isolation of out-workers | Discretion not controlled |
| Use of jargon/complicated language | Rules interpreted rigidly |
| Lack of accountability | No ethos of service |
| Lack of collaboration | 'We know best' |
| Customers fobbed off/passed around | Customer needs not known |
| 'Its not my job' | Impersonal approach |
| Little commitment to training | Limited honest communication |
| Managers use power not motivation | Cynicism |
| Management team don't plan | Autocratic management style |
| Poor/limited management skills | Little or no consultation |
| Complacency | Increasing staff turnover |
| High sickness/absence rates | Poor team spirit |
| Low morale | Few performance standards |
| Constant interference by committee | Awkward customers get best deal |
| No appeal/complaints mechanism | No customer care code |
| Frustration/anger evident | Apathy |
| People do not seem to care | Policy not written down |
| Procedures not followed | Secrecy |
| Low status of front-line workers | Evasive answers |
| Lack of empathy/sympathy | |

It is obvious that such a list contains clear indications about the need for change.

In order to be quite specific about the nature, and use, of surveys in collecting information for use in writing a capability assessment, we are additionally setting out various examples of the survey approach, as they might be applied to different stakeholder groups. Chapter 4 sets out the broad stakeholder groups (p.64). Here we set out a series of surveys to investigate their 'stakes' or interests further, the results of which will establish the basis for change.

## c) Manager's surveys

The first investigates and focuses upon the specific role played by managers within your organisation and might include the following questions and options:

---

Are the values clear and/or explicit?

Is there a vision or clear direction for the organisation?

Is there ssessment of the current achievement of objectives?

Is the departmental structure effective and/or appropriate?

Are roles analysed to establish clarity at all levels within the housing organisation?

What is the extent of participation in management decision-making and policy-making by middle managers and staff?

Is delegation offoctive throughout the organisation?

Is management/leadership style both effective and/or appropriate?

Is there effective teamwork?

Are managers competent and confident?

What are the particular obstacles/barriers to managing staff?

---

As can be seen there is some overlap between the general and specifically targeted surveys and the balance between the two must be carefully struck to avoid undue repetition. But it must also be noted that some repetition may be useful as an internal validation process within the capability assessment process as a whole.

Ansoff (1987) also sets out a useful list of managerial attributes which might be used to measure "general management capability" (Table 13.4, p. 212).

## d) Staff survey

The second survey complements and dovetails into the management survey and looks at the same issues from the staff's point of view. It is important to assure respondents that the information they provide will be treated as confidential, and accordingly questionnaires should be completed anonymously. In terms of representativeness, the general rule is that only a sample, say 50 per cent, is required for those staff who essentially carry out the same tasks. Where there is only one officer carrying out a particular task, which potentially might make their response identifiable, further care must be exercised with respect to confidentiality. The response rates associated with this type of survey are usually high.

With respect to staff surveys, the range of information required is necessarily different as follows (illustratively):

---

What do you think of the organisation now?

Are values clear?

Is the departmental structure adequate and appropriate?

Does the structure facilitate effective working?

Are objectives clear and achievable?

Are staff roles clear and known throughout the organisation?

Are staff encouraged to participate in decision-making?

Delegation arrangements are clear and adequately answers the question – how far can I go within the parameters of the job?

How are staff managed?

Do teams work effectively at all levels within the organisation?

Is there sufficient competency demonstrated within the roles and tasks to be achieved?

Are developmental opportunities available to, and appropriate for, all staff?

---

### e) Other stakeholder surveys
The views of two stakeholder groups – partners and board or committee members need to be sought.

It will also be important to ascertain the perceptions of organisations and agencies with whom you have 'partnership' agreements The term **partners** is used in a wide sense to describe any organisations who have regular and detailed dealings with your housing organisation.

The importance of this kind of survey is to gather information about the external perceptions of the organisation under review. The relevant partners and agencies will vary according to the type of housing organisation. Examples are as follows:

*Housing Associations*
Regulatory bodies (Housing Corporation/Welsh Office/Scottish Homes)
National Housing Federation/Welsh and Scottish Federation of Housing
Associations

Managing partners
Lenders
Contractors
Consultants

*Local Authorities*
Other local authority departments, e.g. social services, economic development
Housing associations
Partner agencies (including health authorities)

Accordingly, in discussion with those with whom the organisation has most
contact, draft a semi-structured questionnaire including the following questions
(and integrate the answers with the management/staff surveys):

---

Are your and their aims/objectives understood?

Are they achieved?

Are there any difficulties/obstacles in the relationship?

What are future expectations?

---

The prime objective is to gain insights into what strengths and weaknesses these
agencies have identified when dealing with the organisation under review. These
perceptions can be built into recommendations for change, such as strengthening
relationships or dealing with barriers and obstacles to successful partnership
arrangements. There is always valuable information to be collected from such a
survey.

In addition, visit partners/agencies to gather further agreed, and perhaps more
detailed information. All this information should be subsequently collated into a
short report.

**Committee and board members:** in discussion with others (as above), draft a
semi-structured questionnaire (committee members are an obvious target group)
including:

**Committees**

(Source documentation for housing associations)

Relevant Housing Corporation/Welsh Office checklists

NHF Code of Governance

(Questions for all committees)

**Background and experience:**

–  Why are you on the committee? For how long?

**Your role on the committee now:**

–  What would you wish it to be?

**Values/vision/aims/objectives of organisation understood:**

–  Do you get sufficient information etc. from managers?

**Confidence level in your managers:**

–  What do you think about the organisation effectiveness?

–  Do you understand the functions of the various departments?

**Relationship between housing committee/management committee and sub-committees:**

**Roles and accountability of the various sub-committees (if any):**

–  Are objectives achieved?

**Efficiency and effectiveness:**

–  Are achievements monitored?

–  How are the relationships to be improved?

As above it may be necessary to visit individuals in order to gather further agreed information. Again collate the information into a short report.

The above outline refers to the relevant committees of housing associations and local authorities and suggestions have already been made as to the source material for the semi-structured questionnaire. The main objective is to obtain the perceptions and comments of the respective policy makers as to their roles and their effectiveness. Research has discovered that there may be varying ideas about what these roles might, or ought to be, and clarification can be obtained by careful documentation. It is also important to ascertain whether the direction, values and objectives of the organisation are known and understood. No prior assumptions should be made when collecting this type of information. Other important aspects are the range and sufficiency of monitoring information obtained from senior managers and their general understanding of the functioning of the organisation. There may be sub-committees and the relationship between these and the main committee should be explored.

### f) Customer surveys
It is useful to appraise information arising out of the previous work as a starting point and, collating information already available about customers' views regarding:

---

What range of services are required and what is the usage of existing services?

What are their expectations?

How does the organisation live up to them?

What are their future expectations?

What monitoring is there of performance to customers?

---

### g) Satisfaction surveys
Information about the views of customers may come from a variety of sources – complaints; enquiries through formal channels; comments at tenants' meetings and so forth and all such data must be analysed. Many housing organisations have taken to conducting regular surveys about customer satisfaction. The emphasis here, however, is rather wider in terms of:

- finding out about, and actually providing, the services which customers require (this may also be related to the service demand analysis since there is little point in providing services which are not used or which can be provided in other ways at less cost);
- matching the right services to needs of customers;
- discovering the levels of customer satisfaction with existing services (provide broad indications only).

As mentioned in connection with the last point, such surveys need to be capable of pin-pointing organisational issues which require attention in order to increase tenant and customer satisfaction, the provision of future services, the re-targeting or development of existing services and guidance suitable for the strategic development of thc organisation.

There are some difficulties about measuring service in this way, which may also limit the usefulness of such information in providing data about the organisation itself. This is partially connected to the type of survey used, of which there are four: exit; postal; random and selected door-to-door polls. Much depends on the *content* and *type* of question asked and the *length of the interview*.

**Exit polls** are short surveys conducted immediately after service users have visited your offices. They provide immediate feedback on their reactions to service delivery arrangements. But it is only possible to have a narrow focus, given the limited time available and breadth of service being surveyed (the immediate service being sought by the customer). They can only measure satisfaction levels within the immediate range of experience and with relatively few questions, since the time tolerance level will be low. It must also be taken into account that users may have been accessing a number of services simultaneously and a question must therefore be asked about the nature of the service(s) sought.

**Postal surveys** also require succinct and short questions, usually in a multi-choice format in order to increase what is usually a poor response rate. The questioning range is again limited to few and very general questions.

**Door-to-door surveys** allow more time for a wider range of questions to be asked. It is also possible in a longer face-to-face interview to highlight the main areas of satisfaction and/or concern, and to ask follow-up questions for clarification purposes – even though these must be tightly controlled for standardisation and comparability purposes. A wider range of questions can be used to target and elicit responses about key services and issues. People are also generally prepared to spend more time answering such questions in the comfort of their own home.

Some of the factors to be taken into account with such surveys may be summarised as follows:

- the cost and time of carrying out such surveys;
- limitations as to breadth and scope;
- offers, such as prizes, used to maximise response rates;
- selected samples may tend to draw upon a relatively small sample of opinion, which may or may not represent the views of all customers;
- the questions to be asked must be clear and simple to answer, where there is limited time or little incentive to respond;
- ensuring door-to-door interviewers are trained in interviewing techniques to ensure objective recording of responses from the customer – for instance, no leading questions;

- ensuring that the data is processed accurately and consistently;
- possible apathy on the part of respondents if previous surveys have not been acted upon.

There is, of course, the option of engaging external researchers to carry out such surveys.

Such surveys rarely provide a useful picture about the internal functioning of a housing organisation, the strategic development of the service, information about the provision of future services or the re-targeting of existing services. These issues are crucial to organisational analysis and strategic planning and management (and the management of change).

There is also the question of the interpretation of the survey results, which tend to be shown as gross percentages of 'satisfaction' or 'dissatisfaction' about each service area without being able to precisely identify what may be wrong. This is a particular drawback of the postal survey, which can only hope to paint a very broad picture indeed.

Whilst **narrative** data is more difficult to code and input, such information may prove to be far more useful as evidence for the need for change as is required by a capability assessment. More informal methods are therefore to be encouraged and provide much more information about the organisation itself.

Senior managers may consider, as with the focus groups for staff (see later), setting up informal/ad-hoc meetings with associations/groups.

Questionnaires may either be used alone, with no face-to-face contact with the respondent or form the basis of a semi-structured face-to-face interview. The disadvantage of the former method is that it is obviously impossible to ask follow-up questions, which may clarify comments about the organisation. It is, however, possible to compare the answers obtained since the same questions are put to all, or a representative sample, of managers and staff. It is desirable to have a separate questionnaire for managers and staff, since the issues and questions to be raised will be different.

Fitzgeorge-Butler (1992d) provides a useful summary of the merits of the different types of survey method (exit, postal, and face-to-face polls). But it might be useful to supplement survey methods with methods to collect the anecdotal experiences of customers with respect to problems about, or deficiencies within, service provision. Informal meetings with individual or groups of tenants can provide such opportunities, and much more detail about existing services – how customers might wish services to be provided in the future, especially if used in a fundamental review for Best Value (see Fitzgeorge-Butler, 1997). Such narrative information is more difficult to encode and analyse and there may be some problem with perceived objectivity and the possible naming of individual officers. But they do provide more detail about what precisely needs to be rectified and it is therefore worth the effort to collect, analyse and interpret this kind of data.

### h) Time log surveys

Time logs are a different type of survey in that they attempt to discover the 'unit times' of the elements of work comprising housing tasks. The following methodology has been found useful for determining these unit times (and subsequently the unit costs of housing organisations):

---

Use the mapping results to draw up elements of all tasks/activities carried out.

Identify categories of analysis for time logs – subject areas (allocation), activities (interviewing, using VDUs) and locations.

Draw up time logs for similar/specific areas of activity.

Completion of time logs by managers and staff – one day per week for five weeks (avoiding unusual weeks etc.).

Analysis of time logs to identify unusual variations for similar tasks/activities – Investigate.

Analysis of time logs to identify unit costs/costs for specific types of activity.

Apply labour costs to unit time to develop unit costs.

Amend for levels of decision-making – too high/too low (will affect unit costs).

Aggregate unit costs for costs per activity.

---

### i) Service demand surveys

Yet another type of survey will provide information about the demand for services at the various service delivery points – telephone, reception desks and so forth. This particular activity is important because of the need for accurate information about the use of particular services as follows:

---

Time logs will provide some information about volume.

Establish measures of volume from existing sources.

New/effective/cost effective methods of measuring/monitoring volume.

Existing service delivery methods effective – any new methods.

Standards for existing services – Customer Care codes etc.

Targets set and achievable.

---

## j) Analysis of surveys

The results from any of the types or variant of survey used will need to be collated in order to provide a coherent picture of the functioning of the organisation and can be accomplished as follows:

Collection of completed questionnaires.

Analysis in terms of common cultural/operational patterns.

Short reports written summarising the management and staff surveys.

Agreement on what information to divulge to focus groups to assist their deliberations.

Identification of any immediate or urgent action which cannot wait for the final report.

It is necessary for an organisation to be fully committed to the time and effort required to carry out and analyse such surveys since the latter task may require substantial resources.

## 5. Diagnostic interviews

Such an interview is more free flowing and unstructured than the questionnaire approach and is based on a counselling approach to organisational analysis. The general aims are to assist with the diagnosis of interpersonal problems within your organisation, and identifying personal development and training needs. One use is when a manager is attempting to diagnose the root causes, and extent, of a particular, and usually known, issue or problem facing members of staff or supervisors.

It is also necessary to exercise care with the giving and receiving of feedback when using this method. The reason for this is that such interviews usually produce highly sensitive information about the organisational culture, some of which may be hidden from managers. It must therefore be collected with care and, because of its confidential nature, usually used in an non-attributable form. It is also likely that, from such a source, the need for a more thorough organisational survey will be identified.

The following method has been found to be a useful and successful approach for gathering such relatively sensitive information:

- Work in pairs – one acting as interviewee, one as an interviewer (for developmental purposes you might work in trios with a third person acting as an observer). Each person will have the opportunity to act in each of the above roles.

- Keep the interview as informal as possible.

- Ensure confidentiality and anonymity.

- The interviewer asks 'open' questions and solicits information from the interviewee about the organisation in general and any specific personal difficulties or problems being experienced. *Solutions must not be discussed.*

- Interviewers should listen and talk as little as possible (just ask questions).

- The interviewer should summarise what has been agreed at regular intervals.

- Towards the end of the interview the interviewer may be asking more closed questions to ensure joint understanding of the issues covered.

**Illustrative example – Questions for investigating management style**

What does your manager do when things go wrong?

How often does your manager praise you?

Do they tell you if you are doing well?

What happens at team meetings?

Is the way your manager deals with you appropriate for your learning and development?

The success of this method of collecting information is contingent on a number of important factors. Namely, the use of an appropriate (reflective) questioning technique; building up a rapport with the interviewee; the use of non-committal 'lubricants' (nods, eye contact and so forth which indicate active listening); and the use of simple, uncomplicated questions and language (multiple-questions are particularly unhelpful). Certainly, questions which elicit a yes or no response are unsuitable for a diagnostic interview. The interviewer therefore concentrates on listening, probing and clarifying, until the nature of the issue or difficulty is known.

Appraisal interviews are a variant of the diagnostic interview and also assist with the diagnosis of the nature of the organisation and its culture with a view to slowly changing personal behaviour over time. One important distinction is that it is appropriate to offer solutions in an appraisal interview, whereas, in a diagnostic interview, it is not.

## 6. Personal observation

Although not an important method of analysis, and a particularly subjective one at that, it should be remembered that we all carry around perceptions about our organisations in our minds. Although some of the specific exercises and methods mentioned in this chapter are designed to verbalise such ideas, those who plan and carry out the capability assessment will inevitably have their own perceptions too. These should not be discounted entirely, but used in an intelligent way to assist the investigation process through expressing ideas as to where difficulties *might* lie and, perhaps, where particular types of evidence might be found. Such ideas cannot be taken as correct assumptions unless corroborative evidence is discovered.

After all, it is the formal and objective recording of personal observation, from a wide range of people, which is at the heart of this process. However, the collected information is being used to build up organisational and cultural patterns about the organisation, which will be recognised, albeit reluctantly by some, if not all organisational members.

## 7. Identification of training needs

This method is included because of the unusual opportunity it presents for collecting, often inadvertently, information which is often similar in content to that available from the interview or questionnaire approaches. It has been found that comments about the organisation have been offered gratuitously when the training needs of managers and staff are being discussed individually. The reason for this is not difficult to comprehend since the strengths and development needs of individual managers and staff are closely related to the needs of the organisation as a whole. Training needs reflect perceived weaknesses within the organisation.

It can therefore be seen that *any* relatively informal interview with managers or staff on almost any topic will produce useful data for organisational analysis, especially when people are relaxed. Usually, however, it will be found that such information is of a negative character since it represents organisational features which obstruct individuals doing their job. They might comment on such matters as:

-    the management style of their supervisor;
-    how they would like to be more involved in decision-making;
-    how team meetings go;
-    information which they needed to know, but did not;
-    inappropriate working methods and environment.

It is useful for those planning to investigate training need analyses to ask more specific questions about the organisation and its culture, obstacles to improvement and so forth. Another important aspect is how people *feel* about their organisation, since problems and issues are sometimes as much about feelings as facts. As with the diagnostic interviews, training needs interviews are not suitable for generating solutions.

## 8. Information from training courses

Similar information to that collected for training needs is often to be gleaned from training events, again whatever the subject. As mentioned above, when participants are relatively relaxed, in an informal setting, managers and staff will discuss their concerns, irrespective.

This source of additional information about an organisation must again be collected and used with caution. Trainers should be open about why and how such information is being collected and used. Such opportunities arise on training courses because there is more time for discussion by managers and staff about the more general issues facing the organisation, even though a different subject may be under discussion. For example, a course on interviewing techniques might elicit comments about the levels of support given to staff facing difficult interviewing situations, the attitude of managers generally and perhaps the lack of facilities for interviewing customers privately. Trainers should collect this information on a separate piece of flipchart paper during the course and hand it on to either managers or those conducting the position statement analysis at the conclusion. It must be emphasised that trainers must state clearly that this is being done and why.

If such information were collected as a matter of course, managers would have useful access to recurrent information about their housing organisation. It is, however, not being suggested that any specific time be devoted to this task, and indeed it would be counter-productive to do so.

## 9. Discussion and focus groups

The objectives of this method are to identify issues and problems facing the organisation by gaining a consensus within a group setting. The initial task is to encourage the group to 'brainstorm' as wide a range of possible organisational issues as possible. There should be no evaluation of these issues at this stage. Such discussions are essentially a 'mapping' exercise where group members individually survey the possible range of organisational difficulties being experienced.

As to the methodology, each item should be discussed in turn. The comments and responses of the group are noted by the group leader, especially items on which there is broad agreement. The variation in, and the contrasts between, the responses are the raw data from which evidence may be drawn to illustrate the issues facing each service area and about the strengths, weaknesses and culture(s) of the organisation.

Discussion groups are not an appropriate forum to raise the strengths and development needs of individuals. Rather, attention should be paid to the aggregate strengths and weaknesses of the organisation and it is these which are to be recorded. Discussion groups can be seen to be an extended version of the SWOT analysis and discussions might begin with such an exercise, or the results from one.

Focus groups with generic/specialist teams may concentrate on the findings from a survey analysis: is there anything missed/to be added/or further thoughts on the current position?

Such groups of managers and/or staff will allow organisational analysts to gain a sense of what is happening within the organisation that is based more on anecdotal examples of difficulties and problems rather than research methodology. The method is, however, valid since it allows groups to comment on, and flesh out, preliminary findings from the surveys with actual examples, usually unattributed, but useful nonetheless.

There are some potential difficulties such as staff being unwilling to speak freely in the presence of managers. In such cases it is usual to engage the services of an external facilitator or to utilise a member of the corporate services group (training officers) in leading such groups of staff. This facilitation role is important since, as the method suggests, groups must be focused on the task.

The following questions should also be addressed:

> What is the precise remit of your focus groups?
> What is the optimum composition of these groups?

Some examples of the kinds of issues which have been addressed by focus groups are as follows:

---

- Management styles (how managers operate either effectively or ineffectively).
- Typical organisational difficulties such as unclear, or lack of adherence to, policies and procedures.
- Delegation methods.
- Effectiveness, or not, of training and development opportunities for staff.
- Mismatches between what the organisational values say and what the organisation actually does.
- Whether staff are motivated or not and how this might be improved.
- What support staff need as opposed to what they actually receive.
- How conflicts and disagreement is managed within the organisation.
- The treatment received by customers on a day-to-day basis (might indicate the need for a Customer Care Code which goes further than the charm school approach).

---

Although Kreuger (1994) discusses focus groups primarily as a research method, and we have used a definition which is altogether more loose, he does very usefully point out when they should *not* be used. Namely, as follows:

- where the environment is emotionally charged;
- when it is not possible to maintain control over the process;
- when statistical projections are required (focus group results are qualitative in nature);
- when other methods can produce better quality information;
- when confidentiality cannot be assured.

In discussions with key members of management staff about effectiveness, information about the following areas may be required:

---

Are policies adhered to?

Are procedures adhered to?

Are there comments on the effectiveness of working methods/possible improvements?

Is decision-making effective at appropriate levels of delegation to managers and staff?

Are standards set *and* achieved?

What constitutes a quality service?

What are particular areas of difficulty etc.?

Any other matters they wish to raise?

---

## 10. Content analysis of documents and published material

This method of analysis involves collecting sets of documents relating to each service area and analysing them according to some agreed criteria. An example of this method is the Plain English campaign, which attempts to increase the level of public comprehension of forms and other published material – cutting out 'jargon', quasi-technical and legal terms. It is, however, important to apply the same, standardised criteria to all the samples under review.

Such material may cover a wide range of documents, such as: application forms; associated explanatory material; summaries to be provided under s.106, Housing Act 1985; committee reports; internal reports; standard and other letters sent to the public; and any other printed material.

The most interesting documents from the point of view of organisational analysis tend to be internal material, not intended for public scrutiny. This data often reveals the 'hidden' cultures of housing organisations – the mismatches between what is published and what housing officials *actually* do.

### 11. Managerial experiences on the front line

Some senior managers have taken to spending time in a front-line position on a regular basis and this may provide useful information about how services are delivered *in practice*. They hear comments about delivery and complaints first-hand.

# Writing the capability assessment report

It can be seen that the amount of information collected may be very large and will require some organising principles in order to make sense of the results. It has been recommended that short reports be produced at the conclusion of each section of analysis – what the SWOT analyses have produced; the broad conclusions of the stakeholders, managers and staff survey and so forth. You will, however, be looking for answers to two key questions, namely:

- What does not appear to be working well?
- What organisational changes might be made to improve the functioning of the organisation?

Typical problems which we have found have included top-heavy management structures, roles of some posts ill defined, failures within communication systems, a lack of control over costs, personal management difficulties, staff with poor standards and lacking in motivation. But patterns will inevitably begin to appear within the data which has been collected.

It is good practice to write a final report at the end of the position statement which sets out the general results of the different analyses together with specific points and suggestions for possible improvements and some overall conclusions from the exercise. Although this chapter has referred to two types of report for Best Value (the overview and fundamental review) it is obvious that the former will be much shorter, and lacking in the detail (and hard facts) of the latter. It is important to be very careful about the interpretation of the limited data on which the overview will be based. For example, will the overview report provide a fair reflection of the functioning of quite complex departmental or business unit work? By contrast, one of the likely difficulties with data emanating from the fundamental review will be the interpretation of the mass of, often conflicting, information.

These reports and statements should be of a general nature and under no circumstances should individuals be named. This is sometimes difficult when units are both unique and small – the comments are easily recognisable. But the objective is to encourage change, not to blame people for past shortcomings.

There are no hard and fast rules about how to write a capability assessment, and even what it might contain, but an important principle must be to clearly identify the **root cause(s)** of problems, in that there may be many symptoms of the same problem. One root cause, say, may be the recent and past history of an organisation and it is important, under such circumstances to identify what went wrong, how it affected the organisation and also perhaps its public image. The cause(s) may have been an inappropriate use of power, a 'laissez-faire' kind of organisation (not much direction and purpose), a paternalistic culture (the organisation or senior managers know(s) best) or over-commitment to professional ideals, which could not deliver the desired outputs. Diagnosis is therefore a very important facet of the review process.

The report must also clearly identify **what needs to change** – say, more direction and a clearer purpose; clarification of management and staff roles; improved morale (even under the constraints of scarce resources) or the creation of a flatter management structure.

Both the overview and fundamental review must also state why it is necessary to make the identified changes, and provide the evidence. Individual summaries of the findings, and interpretations, of the individual surveys and other diagnostic work can be provided in appendices to the main report.

## Format

It is usual to have the full report, with all the appendices, complemented by both an executive summary and a longer summary (no appendices) for all staff and stakeholders, which contains the main points. The full report should always be available if people wish to read or consult it.

It is also important for the reports to be written in comprehensible language and free of management jargon.

The full report may either be written as a chronological statement of the results and findings from each of the diagnostic activities and surveys or in a more analytical format linking the patterns emerging from all the surveys and diagnostic work. Some aspects hang together naturally such as all the external perspectives about the authority and the financial analyses. For clarity, in terms of explaining why changes need to be made, the latter is perhaps more helpful but is more difficult to write. It is also possible to write a chronological account as the work proceeds and use it as the basis for the analytical interpretations and explanations of the patterns.

It will be useful to state why the capability assessment is being undertaken and its specific objectives. Some people will need to clearly understand why it has been undertaken. A statement of the work undertaken prior to the review will also be important for contextual purposes – perhaps the background and meaning of Best Value; the values (guiding principles of the organisation) and their importance; work on identifying customer needs and wants; the purpose, direction and vision for the authority and so forth. This will place the recommended changes in context in order to achieve the vision more effectively.

## The capability statement

This summarises the overall results as to what the organisation does best and what it does not do so well. **General capability** may be deduced from the SWOT analysis results. This may be linked to general difficulties experienced in the past (lack of accountability; uncontrolled discretion; inconsistency) and some indication of the anticipated barriers and obstacles to change (failure to deliver key outputs; negative attitudes and the like). The latter point may be further illustrated by indications from the surveys and other work (it depends what you have asked). External perceptions will also provide further material such as the extent of collaboration and co-operation with other agencies and past responsiveness to citizens and service users. The comments of elected members or management committee may also be included.

There will also be capability statements about particular departments and business units, which support the general capability statement and conclusions. These are conclusions as to present (and to some extent past) capability and might include such subjects as:

- effectiveness of policies, procedures and practices;
- achievement of existing objectives – if not, why not?
- achievement of existing targets and performance standards – both those set by regulatory bodies and internal measures;
- effectiveness of current working methods;
- conclusions from the analysis of the costs of providing existing levels of services;
- the present organisational culture – how it links to the values and its appropriateness.

Any and all statements and conclusions must be fair, backed up with supporting evidence. The bottom-line is that these conclusions are based on what customers, other external stakeholders, elected members, managers and staff have told you.

## Recommendations for change

These recommendations are completely dependent on the results of the capability assessment but might include the following:

- elected members or management committee members providing more direction;

- communicating the direction and vision to employees more effectively;
- more and better strategic planning by the corporate centre;
- more visibility for senior managers;
- changing management styles – more participative, less autocratic;
- more co-operation and collaboration between departments;
- clearer objectives and targets;
- training for staff and managers which is linked to the achievement of organisational objectives;
- more participation in decision-making;
- more regular team briefings;
- set up continuous review facilities.

The focus for change is not change for change sake but to improve the internal functioning of the organisation to better serve the requirements of citizens and service users. Further, the answers to these and other possible questions, posed by the report, is probably best resolved through initial consideration by the management team and further consideration, where appropriate within existing teams. The agreed values will be a good guide as to which answers the organisation might consider appropriate and which not. But it is of paramount importance that specific and precise conclusions be drawn about where and what change is required with clear recommendations made about what might be done about it.

## Summary and conclusions

This chapter has set out to both explain the need for a capability assessment before embarking out on a change process and the tools required to accomplish it. There are different ways of looking at this aspect of managing change but most authors point to the need to link the assessment of the current state of your organisation to the complete process.

In terms of actually drawing up a capability assessment, there are a wide range of tools of which some are formal – for example, surveys – and others more anecdotal – picturing the organisation and observations, for instance. But many kinds of evidence are required to ensure that the most accurate statement of where you are now is possible. It is very useful to identify clusters of change problems and the readiness and capability of relevant subsystems within your organisation.

There is a useful diagram in Beckhard and Harris (1987) which more or less links the whole process with the capability assessment (p 69). However, the key issue is the comparison between where you are now and where you wish to be. This important process should ultimately clearly identify what you need to change to achieve your overall goal.

# Further reading

Ansoff, I. (1987) *Corporate Strategy*, Update Edition, Penguin, Harmondsworth.

Beckhard, R. and Harris, R.T. (1987) *Organisational Transitions: Managing Complex Change*, Addison-Wesley, Wokingham.

Bowman, C. and Asch, D. (1987) *Strategic Management,* Macmillan, London.

Faulkner, D. and Johnson, G. (1992) *The Challenge of Strategic Management*, Kogan Page, London.

Fitzgeorge-Butler, A. W. (1992a) *Analysing Culture*, Absolutely Essential Management of Housing Series, Milton Keynes.

Fitzgeorge-Butler, A. W. (1992b) *Analysing Your Organisation*, Absolutely Essential Management of Housing Series, Milton Keynes.

Fitzgeorge-Butler, A. W. (1997) *Best Value: A Strategic Framework*, Absolutely Essential Management Series, Milton Keynes.

Grundy, T. (1993) *Implementing Strategic Change: A Practical Guide for Business*, Kogan Page, London.

Hofer, C. W. and Schendel, D. (1978) *Strategy Formulation: Analytical Concepts*, St Paul, Minnesota: West.

Jackson, P. and Palmer, R. (1989) *First Steps in Measuring Performance in the Public Sector*, Public Finance Foundation, London.

Krueger, R. A. (1994) *Focus Groups*, Sage, London.

Thompson, J. L. (1997) *Strategic Management: Awareness and Change*, 3rd Edition, International Thomson Press, London.

Warner Burke, W. (1982) *Organisation Development: Principles and Practices*, Scott Foresman and Company, London.

# CHAPTER 6:
# Where are we going?

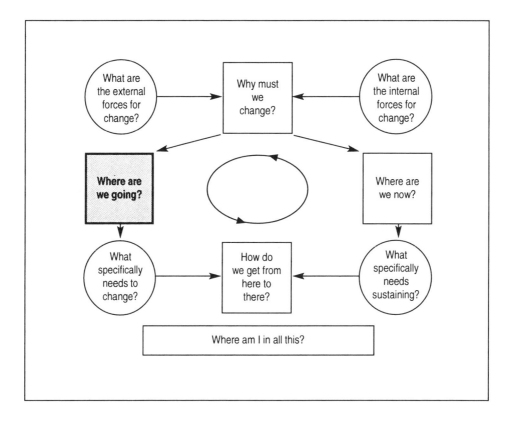

What are the external forces for change? → Why must we change? ← What are the internal forces for change?

**Where are we going?**

Where are we now?

What specifically needs to change? → How do we get from here to there? ← What specifically needs sustaining?

Where am I in all this?

**Objectives**
After reading this chapter you should have:

- recapped on the pressures for change;
- considered some of the options for dealing with those pressures;
- examined one model for undertaking a strategic review;
- briefly considered how mission statements and measures of success fit into this process.

# Introduction

Where are we going? If only we knew? This might well be the answer you offer although some of those reading this chapter will have a very clear idea of where they intend their organisation to be. As this implies, we should not assume everybody is confused about the future even though many of us are!

In part, the answer to the question will depend upon who is being asked the question. Some readers may be thinking of answering in terms of personal destinations. Plans for promotion, to change jobs, to retire, may be well advanced and regardless of the prospects for the organisation, the individual concerned is 'well set'. Our concern here is, however, with respect to the future of housing organisations. Personal futures are part of that, and at times can be very influential on what happens to the organisation as a whole, but the future for individuals is not the focus here.

In Chapters 2 and 3 we set out the forces of change. The focus of this chapter is on destinations. In essence, it is concerned with what we hope to achieve by changing and, in broad terms, how we might change. It should be stressed that it is not possible in the space of one chapter to cover all the possibilities. As will be clear from current debates in the lead-up to the outcomes of the comprehensive spending review in housing a wide range of ideas are now being canvassed and each week a new variant gets press coverage. What this all suggests is that housing organisations are very actively thinking about their futures. This chapter will really serve as an 'aide mémoire' to some of those debates and the earlier material covered in Chapters 2 and 3. It then goes on to examine the process of generating options and reviewing them as part of a strategic review. The overall aim is to get you to think about the future and to provide a means of evaluating the different options.

# The changing environment

Housing organisations are responding to a range of pressures. These emanate first from within the organisation itself and second from external pressures, that is within the housing system and broader social and economic trends and of course from government. The change of government in May 1997 has not reduced many of these pressures. Indeed, in some senses it has exacerbated them not least by the sense of uncertainty as to what might be the final direction of policy. The focus here will be on the external pressures.

*The pressures from within the housing system include:*

- High levels of homelessness, albeit that recently overall numbers have declined.

- The ever tighter targeting of social housing to those most in need.
- Lack of investment in the existing social housing stock, again although this varies considerably between organisations.
- The loss of stock through the right-to-buy and other initiatives and the constraints this brings in terms of opportunities to move into and within social housing.
- Coping with policy changes and the implications of policy, e.g., for local authorities – the retention of Housing Management Compulsory Competitive Tendering (HMCCT) and the development of the replacement Best Value regime, and for housing associations – rent policy, tax relief grant changes, cuts in housing benefit for supported housing, rising costs of new development.
- Continuing problems in the home ownership market, e.g., arrears and possessions leading to extra pressures on social housing providers in terms of advice and assistance.
- Affordability and the cost of housing under the high rent regimes required by the previous government. While this has now changed, the consequences remain.
- The cutbacks in and the weaknesses of the housing benefit system, not least the difficulty of obtaining work while retaining benefit.

*Beyond housing, pressures include:*

- The general downward pressure on public resources leading to cuts in capital and revenue budgets, declining public provision of services and growing privatisation of social welfare. While the change of government perhaps reduces these pressures it has retained the expenditure limits previously set and thus operates in a somewhat similar way. The release of capital receipts for use by local authorities is not insignificant but in reality the need for new resources to deal with a backlog of neglect is very great indeed.
- Increased job mobility and geographic mobility, less security of income and more specifically the high levels of unemployment among social housing tenants and the limited opportunities to move on (either within the stock or to homes in the private sector).
- Growing problems of security, crime, vandalism, the loss of social cohesion and the break down of local communities.
- Demographic change leading to more older people, more single people and fewer traditional families, even though the UK has a system which is best structured to assist the last.
- Community Care and support for those with a range of 'special' needs.
- Employment change to contract and more temporary jobs, more female work.
- The growth in the number of refugees/asylum seekers.

- Intense competition for resources and increasingly for market share within the social rented sector.
- The rise of individualism and consumerism.
- The increasing use of private solutions which generate public costs.
- Questions of sustainable consumption; energy, water, land, materials.
- Land availability, NIMBYISM, and transportation issues.
- Changes in technology and its impact upon homes, jobs and human relationships.
- A general problem of urban governance and the relationships between local areas and central government together fuelling a growing fiscal problem.

If these are at least some of the pressures you would identify (and there will always be others which are specific to your organisation) then how might we respond to them? Or indeed do we need to respond to them? Can't we just ignore them and carry on as we are? Or aren't some such big issues there is nothing to be done?

The simple answer is yes, you can ignore them but there will be consequences. It is perhaps relevant to remind readers that this is a book about strategic management. It is concerned with managing and developing organisations over the long term and through an environment which is often turbulent and never or at least rarely stable.

Having said this the pressures for change will be felt differentially. This will be influenced by the size, role and location of the organisation and its capacity and potential to absorb and manage the pressures upon it. For example, a small almshouse housing association with no development programme may be fairly insulated from much of what goes on. In contrast, a large regional or national housing association may feel the pressures much more but may also have the capacity to respond to them, whether through adaptation or some other strategy. Going further, a large urban local authority will probably be under greater pressure than a small rural authority. It will almost certainly have a more difficult management task and it will probably be much more exposed to criticism whether it be from tenants, the public in general or politicians.

## Responding to change

Certainly, there are a range of choices for housing organisations about how to respond to change. At an organisation structure level, the choices for a social housing organisation might include some of the following:

- stay as we are;
- adapt and change;

- transfer stock;
- merge with another housing association;
- be taken over by another housing association;
- let others take over (e.g., tenants or private company);
- various variants on the above;
- withdraw from the market and change role.

However, depending upon the pressures and the impacts they are having, most of the above might be seen as unnecessary responses. Even though one might at least ask some of these questions, the answer to most problems will be to deal with them within the confines of the existing organisation structure and arrangements. Our concerns are primarily with issues which test in one way or another the capacity of the organisation. As we stated at the start of this book our primary concerns are with the question of the management of strategic change. A recent Housing Corporation report, *The Future of Independent Social Housing* is a useful review of some of the issues (Housing Corporation, 1997a)

Let us examine this further through examples. First, if growing pressures on the rent account are due to growing poverty amongst tenants, the initial solution would not be to merge with another organisation or to withdraw from the market. It should in the first instance be about helping tenants maximise their entitlement to state assistance while at the same time looking closely at the organisation's rent policy. Second, it might be to explore whether there is any potential for cross subsidy from other activities. Third, it could lead to work on assisting tenants to find jobs which would enhance their capacity to pay rents. This in turn might direct the organisation to think more clearly about local sourcing and 'Housing Plus' type agendas (Clapham et al, 1998).

Similarly, if the terms under which new homes were being acquired were so punitive in out-turn rents then the organisation would have to consider whether it was appropriate to continue to do so. Indeed, if it had secured maximum efficiency in terms of its operating costs and it had explored all other means of supplementing grant aid, it might have no other option but to cease acquisition or new build. One option adopted by some associations has been to cross subsidise the rents on new dwellings from increased rents on older dwellings. Not only will this be increasingly difficult under the 'RPI plus 1' policies now coming into place but it does run against the overriding aim of keeping rents low overall in order to reduce the housing benefit trap. As will be apparent there are competing objectives!

Looking ahead, it might take the decision to move into the market rent area and establish a business there with the intention of allowing the profits from that to flow back to the social rented activity in the form of cross subsidy. This might be achieved quickly via the purchase of an existing portfolio of property or it could be built up over time.

For local authorities, choices as to the future have been very starkly posed in recent years. Declining resources have led to local authorities deciding to transfer their stock to housing associations (and most recently to local housing companies), primarily because the latter could raise private finance while the authorities themselves were denied this opportunity by central government. While many authorities have not wanted a house building programme of the scale undertaken in the 1960s and 1970s, it is evident that most, via their waiting lists, have continued to demonstrate a demand for the services they can provide. While associations have been able to provide what in many cases have been very adequate alternatives, there has been a continuing demand for local authority housing (and this is not simply because rents were lower).

Alongside a continuing demand for homes has come an increasing pressure to update and improve the existing stock and to generally enhance the quality of the housing service. Set against a context of dwindling resources, no new homes, the sale of better homes via the right-to-buy and the pressures to improve stock and services, it is no wonder many authorities have undertaken strategic reviews. Such reviews have pointed to the demand pressures upon the authorities and their growing difficulties in supplying adequate housing to meet them. The reviews have stressed the contribution of other sectors and agencies but many have still concluded that resources are insufficient. Transfer and the raising of debt to fund new programmes of upgrading and new building along with access to housing association grant and a private finance regime have been very attractive options.

But of course, as any reader of this book will know, not all authorities have been in a position to sell their stock and gain a capital receipt for re-investment while at the same time passing on an asset against which debt could be raised to finance new activity. For a significant number of authorities their stock could only be sold at a loss (a negative valuation) and they would be required to give the purchaser a dowry of sufficient funds to upgrade what they had sold at a loss. Otherwise there might be no purchaser!

Clearly, this was a non-starter for the authorities concerned. Their best option was often to continue as before and press the government for resources to improve their stock (alongside generating more cash reserves via higher rents and selected disposals). For many authorities the overriding concern has been with their own stock and the pressures and demands that generates.

The creation of the Estates Renewal Challenge Fund (ERCF) was a somewhat cumbersome attempt to lure such authorities to transfer stock and following the debacle of the failed Sandwell transfer the programme is to be re-considered. The problems of ERCF (limited funds, funding competition and the complexities of securing tenant support) has led to work on derivatives from the local housing companies model. The Chartered Institute of Housing put forward the idea of local housing corporations (Hawksworth and Wilcox, 1995) and most recently the Local Government Association has proposed the creation of local housing quasi-corporations (LGA, 1997). These are basically local housing companies inside the local authority (with the local authority retaining ownership). Rather than saddling the new organisation with the cost of transferring the stock, debt is raised against the property assets with a view to the funds raised paying for improvements to the stock. The government has been sympathetic to these ideas and has focused upon evaluating the cost effectiveness of different approaches.

The government has also given a green light to introducing the Private Finance Initiative (PFI) to council housing. Support is being given to a non-Housing Revenue Account scheme in North East Derbyshire and it is hoped PFI can be introduced for housing revenue account activities. In essence, PFI introduces a time limited revenue subsidy which tops up the rental income to service the private debt raised. The supplier of the service faces performance penalties and takes the risk that there will be a demand for the dwellings involved. At the end of the contract the dwellings provided (or refurbished) pass back to the local authority. Again a range of PFI structures are being considered and the relative effectiveness of these is under consideration.

While many authorities have insufficient resources to tackle the problems with their own stock, there has been a general move to embrace a wider 'enabling' role. The previous government's campaign to move local authorities out of direct housing provision and to become enablers who would oversee provision by others was an unfortunate start to something which had many positive attributes. Many authorities had long played a wider role than simply providing their own council homes. For example, Birmingham City has for many years played a major role in private sector renewal activity and in the management of houses in multiple occupation (and most recently has developed a wide ranging partnership programme with the private sector). At the same time, some authorities had not paid any significant attention to other providers and to the role of the home ownership, housing association and private rented sectors, instead focusing all their efforts upon their own role as landlord and provider.

In recent years, most authorities have embraced a wider enabling role and this has been enhanced through concerns with and a new role in Community Care. Recognising that there are a range of different ways of solving the same problem (or indeed of preventing the problem arising in the first place) has been an important step forward for authorities (and associations). It has led authorities to adopt a more pragmatic stance to their own stock and to the balance of costs and benefits which might arise in particular situations. Thus, disposing of stock to developers to secure housing gain through new build on vacant land has been an option for some. For others a renewed focus on cost efficiencies has meant that it has been possible to trim elements within the housing revenue account and spend more on repairs and maintenance. Better planning and management has meant it has also been possible to use existing resources to secure better quality outcomes, for example, more and higher quality repairs.

The list of service improvements made by authorities in recent years is substantial. However, it must be seen against a backcloth of declining resources and worsening conditions. Even in the best run authorities there is at times a sense of only coping and surviving through the next round of negative policy and despite any achievements which can be secured, that the specific service is still in a downward spiral. There has therefore been a sense of only controlling the speed of decline rather than the overall direction.

In many respects, regardless of the government in power there will be a continuing shortage of resources for the social housing sector, and perhaps for housing generally. Housing organisations must therefore make continuing efforts to be creative in the way they think about and use resources. The discussion above gives some sense of the range of options and the NHF publication, *Financing the Future: and anticipating the consequences* (NHF, 1996) very usefully summarises these, primarily for housing associations but also with some applications for local authorities.

## Guiding principles

Are there any guiding principles for making choices? We rarely have a free rein and there will be key concerns which will guide, influence or constrain the choices we make. We may be concerned to ensure that, whatever the outcome, it secures a budget reduction or that with the same resources the number of outputs (however measured) are increased. We may have more specific concerns related to tenant control or equal opportunities. Typically, any single choice will secure other outcomes. There will, of course, be many unintended effects. The strategic choices presented to many housing organisations have been set out earlier.

What guides an organisation to make a specific set of choices will be fairly unique to that organisation reflecting the complex amalgam of financial circumstances, political pressures, social and economic contexts, history and tradition it faces. Even where universal models for change are being proposed, e.g., establishing local housing companies, it is quite clear there will be a wide range of local variants. Those variants will be a product of the 'choices' made locally, albeit within an overall setting which raises key strategic questions about the future of local authority housing services.

In setting out to make choices, housing organisations do need to think about first principles such as what are they trying to achieve. In many cases, organisations won't have given as much thought to this as might at first appear. Indeed, some probably do what they have always done and there may well be a fairly uncritical approach to this. The presumption is that what is done is what is needed. However, times do change. The same problems of poor housing or the lack of housing can be tackled in different ways. Providing council housing is certainly one way, and potentially a good way of tackling these problems but it is not the only way. Moreover, as we now know, simply building homes does not guarantee that all problems are solved. Some homes have been poorly planned and poorly built. Some housing management services are poor and do not deliver what tenants want and need. Increasingly (and somewhat belatedly) it has been recognised that the involvement of the community is vital to securing success and that solutions might lie outside the direct provision of better homes. Simply asserting that it is necessary to go on doing what the organisation has always done is not sufficient. Times change and so do roles.

The same arguments apply to all 'solutions'. Every solution has its strengths and weaknesses and it can be delivered well or poorly. Some would assert that housing associations are superior to local authorities while others would argue the opposite. Both are fruitless arguments. Some local authorities and some housing associations perform well and are very effective, but some authorities and some associations are very poor and very ineffective. There is not one universal solution.

Solutions can rarely be taken 'off the shelf'. They require working up and working through. There will be a need to consider the different ways of tackling the problem at hand. This option appraisal will often take place within an overall strategic review. It is to this we now turn.

## *Strategic review*

There are many models for reviewing organisations but the one below is commonly used albeit in a variety of guises. Before working through it, a couple of caveats are worth bearing in mind. First, although the model is set out sequentially (as in the ordered rational world we might all choose to live in!) it is often the case that ideas linked to the different stages arise in a rather more chaotic fashion. The process can and should be iterative, moving backwards and forwards between the stages. Second, not all the stages may be equally relevant to your needs. In the context of this chapter, stages 1 and 2 are not so relevant. Third, remember that this is a planning and review process. It is a preliminary to actually doing it and as such should not consume too much time or resources. A strategic review might take up to two months with a small number of staff working on it and using a wider group as a sounding board and source of ideas. A consultant might be brought in as an external reference for a couple of days. Moving from strategic review to actually doing it is the subject of the next three chapters.

There are six stages in this strategic review model. In outline they are as follows;

**Stage 1. Purpose and scope: who? why? when? what?**
Why is the review taking place, who wants it, when is it needed by and are there any key parameters?

**Stage 2. Need and current provision: what are the needs and what is currently provided?**
This requires drawing together information on the current situation and crucially taking a view as to whether the outcomes are successful. This means doing more, for example, than matching the number of households and dwellings. Issues of cost, quality and sustainability are also vital. It is also essential that some consideration is given to how these needs might change in the future. Potentially you are planning long term developments and investments. Are they going to be justified?

**Stage 3. Generating options: what could be done?**
Ideas can be generated and options explored to meet the needs and gaps identified. These ideas and options need shaping against the range of constraints (e.g., financial and human resources, policy, the law, politics).

**Stage 4. Devising a preferred option: what should be done?**
Detailed work on the options including an evaluation against outcomes, resources, feasibility and risks. Selecting and making the case and covering all the essential questions and issues.

**Stage 5. Implementation planning: how will it happen? when should it happen?**
Assessment of the implementation issues – programming, resourcing and negotiating the way forward. Developing a realistic and robust approach.

**Stage 6. Monitoring and review: how to assess what might be working/not working?**
Thinking through the monitoring and review mechanisms and defining the scope for managerial action.

Much of this is fairly straightforward. However, it is worth making more detailed comment on stages 3, 4 and 5

## Stage 3. Generating options

Stage 2 will provide the working basis for generating the options. It will set out what is needed now and in the future. Further refinement and clarity will emerge as you work on the options. Stage 3 requires a different way of thinking; rather than being solely analytical it demands curiosity and creativity. How you work on this stage will influence what you come up with.

There are three steps in stage 3.

*(a) Generating a range of options or 'solutions'*
Set aside all but the most immovable constraints and seek to build as wide a range as possible. You can do this by:

- seeking ideas from current users and providers;
- using networks, journals, conferences;
- putting in your ideas (remember no one has the monopoly of knowledge);
- getting away from the office and brainstorming, working on even the wildest ideas;
- thinking the unthinkable, e.g., not providing the service, doubling your service, contracting out;
- bringing together creative and radical thinkers alongside practical problem solvers.

Try and distil down the ideas to a reasonably limited set of options. Some may be variants on a theme. Then equipped with your options move onto the next step.

*(b) Reshape the options against the constraints and implementation issues*
Test and reshape the options asking two key questions:

Can you reshape the options to meet the range of constraints including implementation issues?
Can you get round the constraints to allow the options to move ahead?

As already noted, key areas will be current policy commitments, political agendas, resources – money, people and property, people, management and organisational concerns.

*(c) List what options remain*
Exclude only the seemingly impossible options. In stage 4 you can test them to destruction.

## Stage 4. Preferred option

This stage is at the heart of the review process. It is where the options need assessing against the principal criteria for effectiveness. The following diagram sets out a simple evaluation framework listing the key criteria. You may choose to supplement these. You can fill in the boxes with text and/or rankings (i.e., 1 to 5 but remembering that a high or low score means good or bad depending upon the criteria being assessed).

|  | Option 1 | Option 2 | Option 3 | Option 4 |
|---|---|---|---|---|
| **Outcomes** How well does it meet the required outcomes? |  |  |  |  |
| **Resources** What the main resource demands? |  |  |  |  |
| **Risks** What are the main risks for (a) service delivery (b) financial position |  |  |  |  |
| **Feasibility** What are the main barriers to implementation? Can they be overcome? |  |  |  |  |

## Stage 5. Implementation planning

Having identified a preferred option (or two) you then need to consider their feasibility in terms of implementation. What will it take to implement the change effectively?

There are perhaps three key considerations. First, programming the many complex tasks. Use of a Gantt Chart (basically a matrix of time by tasks) can help sequence plans greatly. Second, the staff resources, and third who you will need to negotiate with and in what sequence (on this point it might be useful to use stakeholder analysis and/or do a force field analysis, see Chapter 9, pp.148, 153).

Before concluding this chapter there are two related but in the context relatively minor areas we want to cover. The first of these is mission statements, and the second, how to measure success.

## Mission statements and strategic vision

Although there is often considerable cynicism surrounding mission statements, these can be useful devices for focusing thinking on what the organisation does or where it is going. Both the process of writing the statement and its subsequent use in publications and presentations can be helpful in focusing staff attention on what they are there to achieve. Clearly a mission statement is simply that. It cannot produce anything by itself but it does express intentions and feeds into the subconscious 'ether' of an organisation. Working on a mission statement might lead to questioning as to where an organisation is going.

Many organisations produce mission statements which simply tell us what they actually do, e.g., 'Our mission is to provide good quality affordable homes'. However, there are a number of weaknesses with such a mission statement. While this is what they do it does not tell them why they do it. Moreover given that mission it could be argued that if they stopped building they had failed in their mission and had no ongoing role. What a mission statement should cover is the underlying reason for being in the business, e.g., 'to enable households on low and moderate incomes to secure good quality affordable homes'. This mission statement offers considerable flexibility. It can be fulfilled in many different ways and it sets out a measurable ambition. As Leach (1996) has shown, mission statements focusing on the 'how and why' feed into vision statements about what an organisation is aiming to achieve over a period of time.

Getting agreement on a mission statement can be time consuming and may be seen as a complete waste of time. In reality that process is about clarifying what the organisation is trying to do and achieving a consensus around that. A limited amount of time spent working up a mission statement is time well spent. Having developed a mission statement it is important to promote it as a corporate statement and to measure activities against it. In other words it should be actively used and not just become an obscure and exclusive statement written in Latin on a heraldic shield (which are, of course, early versions of mission statements!).

## Aims and objectives

With (or without) a mission statement in place, it is crucial that an organisation thinks through its broad aims and detailed objectives. What is it there to achieve? A mission statement gives a one line summary, but a set of broad aims may also be helpful, especially where an organisation has a range of activities and roles. However, even with a broad set of aims there will still be a requirement for an even more detailed set of objectives. These objectives can be attached to specific activities/sections within the organisation.

Again this might all be seen as time wasting. It is clearly the case that many housing organisations have 'accumulated' activities and roles over the years without always thinking through whether they need to be undertaken at all. Formulating aims and objectives can result in very valuable clarifications and a much tighter specification of what an organisation is trying to do. It is clear that some authorities have found that in the process of preparing for HMCCT they have had to go back to basics and ask what are we trying to do and how does X or Y activity fit within that.

## Outcomes

In setting out a mission statement we have set out to achieve something. How do we know when we get there? Can it ever be like we imagined it might be? The world changes, organisations change and the needs to be met change. Someone closely involved with a social housing organisation in the 1950s might have some difficulty recognising such an organisation in the late 1990s. Fundamentally, they are still trying to fulfil the same mission but the way it is being approached is quite different.

## Measuring success

How can we measure success? The reality is that with little thought about what they are there to do some housing organisations have little idea as to whether they have succeeded or failed. The most common and obvious measure of 'success' has been the size of the housing stock. With the sale of stock and with reduced new build, many housing organisations could only conclude they were no longer succeeding. It took some years for organisations to widen their view of success to include a wider set of measures.

Even then there has been considerable resistance to comparative performance measurement based regimes. Housing organisations have rightly been concerned that such regimes could be used to allocate ever scarcer resources and to discriminate between organisations. With genuine concern about the relevance, accuracy and fairness of some measures, performance based regimes have developed slowly. However, it is now clear that a performance based culture has begun to take root.

Most performance measures raise as many questions as they provide answers. Even simple numerical counts of the amount spent or the number of repairs undertaken raise questions about what was counted and why a particular organisation might have a higher figure than another. This has led fairly naturally and inevitably to the ideas of peer groups and benchmarking. Grouping together organisations of a similar sort allows for more useful comparisons and calculating a mean performance for that group sets a benchmark which all should strive to achieve.

Setting targets, whether numerical or not gives a clear signal to all staff. It can however distort an organisation's activities. The focus shifts towards meeting those targets above all else. This can mean that equally important but unmeasured (and even unmeasurable) outcomes are neglected. With ever more concern about the wider benefits of housing management activity (e.g., through 'Housing Plus') there is a danger that measures may narrow the focus at the very time when a wider role is desired.

It should be clear therefore that while it is important to attempt to measure success and to have a clear view of when the organisation is achieving what it needs to there are many pitfalls in the process. It is important that any regime introduced should follow a number of simple guidelines:

- be aware of the costs of measuring success and detailed performance;
- keep it simple and to a minimum;
- try and have uncomplicated measures which are not easily corrupted;
- if a measure is not being used, drop it;
- not all measures need to be collected with the same frequency;
- different measures will have relevance to different levels of the organisation.

The aim is to show what the organisation is achieving and to be able to observe the direction of change, i.e., is performance improving, stable or falling? This will give management insights into the effectiveness of the changes they have made.

## Summary

This chapter has sought to examine how a housing organisation might consider where it is going. This chapter should be read in conjunction with Chapters 5, 8 and 9. The first of these offers ways of establishing where the organisation is now and deals with the tools and the means by which options can be considered. The second offers a 'case study' of all of the techniques involved being applied to a mythical 'typical' organisation. The third helps us to consider how we get from where we are to where we want to be.

There can be no single answer to the question, where are we going? The answers will vary greatly and in some cases, it will be 'nowhere'. It is very evident today that given the continued reduction in resources, the more competitive environment and the pressure for reduced costs some organisations will only 'survive' by merging or disappearing.

The late 1990s and the first decade of the next century will see major changes in the size and structure of housing organisations. It will, for example, be ever harder to maintain a traditional small community based housing association as a directly developing organisation.

This chapter has sought to remind readers of the pressures their organisations will be under and the importance of thinking through what they are trying to achieve and some of the different ways they might go about this. It has set out a model for the strategic review process. Finally, it briefly explored the use of mission statements and the value of trying to measure what is being achieved as part of the process of establishing where you might be going and how you would know if you got there.

## Further reading

Clapham, D. et al. (1998) *From Exclusion to Inclusion*, Hastoe Housing Association, London.

Hawksworth, J. and Wilcox, S. (1995) *Challenging the Conventions: Public Borrowing Rules and Housing Investment*, CIH, Coventry.

Housing Corporation. (1997a) *The Future of Independent Social Housing*, Research Report 25, Housing Corporation, London.

Housing Corporation. (1997b) *Household Trends and Housing Sectors*, Research Report 24, Housing Corporation, London.

Institute for Employment Research. (1997) *Housing, Family and Working Lives*, DETR, London.

Leach, S. (1996) *Mission Statements and Strategic Visions: Symbol or Substance*, LGMB, London.

Local Government Association. (1997) *A New Financial Framework for Local Authority Housing*, LGA, London.

National Housing Federation. (1996) *Financing the Future*, NHF, London.

National Housing Federation. (1997) *Local Housing Strategies*, NHF, London.

# CHAPTER 7:
# What needs sustaining?

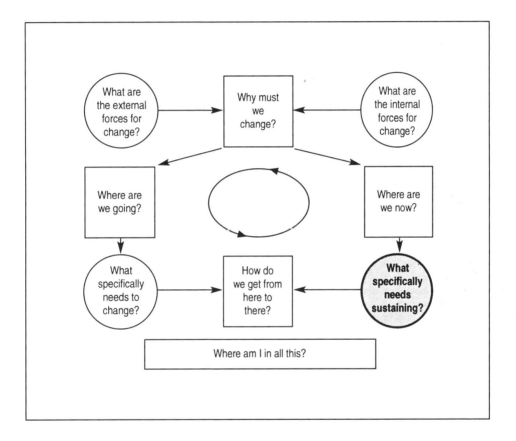

**Objectives**
This chapter will enable you to assess how to sustain your organisation
during a period of major change and specifically to:

- analyse what parts of the organisation need actively sustaining;
- plan how this could happen;
- integrate these plans with those for your major changes.

# Introduction

*"The current pressures for change will make change junkies of us all."*

These were the words of a director who has lived through ten years of continual change. His words reflect a worry that not only will senior managers have to face continual change (the subject of the rest of this book), but that they will actively seek change when things look rather too quiet. There are numerous examples of managers who are restless until they have found something to change. The thrill, as another senior manager put it, of *'shooting the rapids of change'* turns into an addiction. This can detract from the fact that much of the organisation needs managerial effort to sustain its performance.

Why specifically is it so important to sustain an organisation? Our experience of working in many housing organisation suggests there are two key reasons. The *first* is that even with major strategic changes, *a large part of the organisation remains substantially unchanged.* Large sections of the organisation need to continue functioning in a steady way. This means there is a sustaining effort needed if services, systems, structures and people are to continue performing their functions effectively alongside changes. Leadership of change is therefore about the effective handling of both sides of the picture – the parts undergoing planned change, and those which will need varying amounts of support to keep them in a steady state.

The *second* reason is that *it is an active rather than passive process of management.* There is a rather simplistic view of organisations to the effect that anything which isn't actively being changed is therefore static and needs no attention. Observation of any organisation shows that this is not true. For it to be in a steady or stable state is not to say it is static. If individuals and teams are ignored they lose their effectiveness and need maintaining. In addition, organisations are continually moving in an unplanned way. This movement comes, from at least three main sources: the changing environment around the organisation, the ageing of people and the organisation itself, and the internal struggles between people with different perspectives and interests. The changes created by these forces are continually occurring and, as Kantor (1992, p.24) suggests, *"all three occur outside strategic intervention or organisational goals."* Individuals, teams and the organisation need monitoring and any significant changes responding to if the organisation is to be sustained in a steady state.

There is a particularly apt analogy to that of sustaining an organisation, it is that of riding a bike. In order to ride anywhere – the purpose of the bike ride – it is crucial to both maintain the good functioning of the machine and sustain ones balance. Neither happens of its own accord, it needs active attention and action! To say someone is stable on a bike is not to say they are static but rather that they are keeping the machine *performing and balanced*. This idea comes very close to the idea of *sustaining* an organisation in a steady state – ensuring everything is performing in a balanced way.

This *performing and balancing* of any system in a steady state, of which both organisations and bike riders are examples, is sometimes labelled 'homeostasis'. The application of the principle of homeostasis to organisation (Morgan, 1986) draws upon nothing more unusual than ensuring good management practices are used to sustain the healthy running of the organisation. The danger is that these management practices are neglected as the management of change draws the manager's attention away. Hence the need to reiterate the need for sustaining the business – *maintaining its performance and balance* – even when planning a change and a new direction.

This active management process of sustaining the business can be of two kinds; *preventative maintenance* or a *re-direction of resources* to restore balance in the organisation. An example of *preventative maintenance* would be the regular support and recognition that a successful performing maintenance division needs. Individuals and teams are not machines, they need support in maintaining their facilities and equipment, and recognition when successful in meeting targets. An example of the *re-direction of resources* might be an upward movement in rent arrears. Whilst this is not a planned change it does necessitate management action to identify the causes, re-prioritise staff time and action, and set targets to bring the situation back to an acceptable steady state. These all too familiar examples in housing are what we mean by management action which is sustaining the business.

Much of this may seem obvious, and we hope it is, but what does one do about it? It is clearly not focused enough to say that you must keep going with all your good management practices alongside any major change! It needs narrowing down. It is our experience that managers have focused upon three areas – the three 'Ps' – which are particularly important in sustaining the organisation's activities. They are:

- Purpose – clarifying and holding to its purpose and values.
- Performance – monitoring and maintaining its performance.
- People – sustaining its staff.

All three may be areas for major change but when they are not they still require active attention and maintenance. This chapter provides a framework for checking what needs sustaining, and at the end of the chapter, we encourage you to do your own 'sustaining audit' before any major change, to identify how the organisation needs to be actively sustained. Action of this kind will need integrating into your overall change plans. This integration of the management effort, to both change and to sustain the organisation, may prove difficult but is essential for a balanced approach.

# Purpose and values

At the core of any housing organisation are its purpose and values – what it is there to do and what principles and practices it is committed to. Sometimes these are the focus of change, particularly if the organisation is in crisis and requires strategic changes as fundamental as these. For the most part, purpose and values will need active, continuous attention and sustaining. What is important is asking the question: *what needs sustaining?* We consider them separately.

## *Purpose*

One feature of the recent pressures on housing organisations, e.g. CCT on local authority departments or development funding for housing associations, has been the time spent on clarifying the organisation's purpose. At first managers and many staff have, rightly, questioned the need for this, particularly when associated with words like *mission* and *vision* which have smacked of the latest management jargon. Surely the purpose is clear, to provide social housing? Yet many have found that this is not good enough to help them make realistic choices when they are under pressure. Issues necessarily arise such as,

- social housing for what groups?
- with what services?
- to what standards?
- to what areas?
- to grow or retrench?

and many others.

Whilst this can lead to major redefinition it more often than not leads to greater clarity and focus. A focus that needs to be sustained.

An example from a business plan for preparing for housing management CCT, has included two statements, one for the client and one for the contractor side:

On the client side:

> *".... to directly provide or enable provision by other agencies of decent, affordable social housing and to maintain it in a manner wanted by tenants."*

On the contractor side:

> *".... to provide a quality housing management and maintenance service appropriate to specified standards and within budget."*

Each provides a clearer and, because of the CCT separation of client and contractor, narrower statement of purpose for the two parts of the organisation.

Sustaining a more narrow focus in this respect is something that both client and contractor sides are taking time to adjust to, but ironically the work of clarifying it has made the sustaining task easier. Managers on both sides have been used to broader, and, it could be said, woollier definitions of the housing department's purpose. The challenge of CCT preparation, dry running, and managing the contract has encouraged a working to purpose, a sustaining of it and a cutting away of peripheral activities. There have also been many examples of housing associations, in the face of lower grant rates and competition, having to take a hard look at their purpose and deciding to work to sustain a smaller, more focused role.

The key feature of sustaining any organisation in its purpose is the clarity and understandable nature of that purpose. If that is clear, then the task of managing (or sustaining) the organisation so that it keeps *on task* is easier, and there is less chance of that all too frequent phenomenon, *'organisational drift'*, namely taking on interesting but diverting tasks. How clearly focused is your organisational purpose, and is everyone aware of sticking to it?

## Values

We have considered elsewhere how one might assess your organisation's values and how they might need to change (Chapter 5). What about those values that need to be sustained? Increasingly there is a recognition that good values currently held *and* practised within the organisation need actively sustaining. Some examples we have met are of explicitly stating and sustaining the values of:

- Offering a seamless service to the tenant or customer.
- Knowledge and experience of the locality.
- Consistency of quality in delivering routine services.
- Responding to tenants and customers as whole people, and responding to their range of needs.
- Co-operative working between teams (something that tight budgets and CCT can threaten).

All these can be threatened in an environment of change and competition. There needs to be active management to encourage and reward the practice of values that need sustaining. The splitting of organisations into self-contained units, whether client/contractor, cost centres or newly defined businesses within a larger or federal structure, can foster a belief or value that the business unit's operation is all that counts. There is a real danger that 'the new is good and the old is bad', especially if senior managers are the enthusiastic leaders of change. Valued aspects of current practice can be devalued or neglected in the push for changes which are right but not the whole picture.

One way of avoiding this snare is to consider hard and carefully which of the existing organisation's values you want to continue into the new structures.

Recently, in one organisation about to go through a major change, we undertook an exercise called, 'Old Into New', in which we asked the teams:

- Which of your current practices are you committed to take into the restructured organisation?
- What will sustain them?
- How will you monitor any changes?

This proved a very successful way of avoiding the old/new split and reaffirmed (in some cases for the first time) those aspects of the working that teams particularly valued. We would suggest that a similar form of diagnosis *and* supporting action will be necessary in your organisation if it is not to lose the key principles and practices through neglect.

## Performance

If anything is the focus of recent management ideas and attention, it is performance. How can we perform better in terms of the quality, quantity and cost of our services? The twin pressures of competition – performing to competitive quality and cost standards – and reducing budgets – getting the same for less – are hitting most organisations. Housing organisations are no different. For local authorities under CCT and central government funding pressures, and for housing associations with development bidding and Housing Corporation performance criteria, it is no accident that performance dominates much of the manager's time. For many housing organisations, *performance indicators, performance management, performance targets and performance review* are common labels and consumers of time. Whatever the labels, the core activity of any business is its ability to perform to viable targets.

Performance usually receives most attention when it drops below agreed standards, e.g. rent arrears are excessive, or when drastic improvement are required, e.g. benchmarking of costs under CCT competition reveals high overheads. It requires, however, regular and detailed attention and is an essential part of any organisation which requires sustaining. The primary activity with regards to performance is sustaining the regular, repeatable, day-to-day delivery of services to a quality standard and cost.

Every organisation must have a system for defining, forecasting and reviewing service performance. Performance has many qualities of self regulation or homeostasis, i.e. checking how we are doing and taking action to bring the organisation back into a 'steady state'. We believe this characteristic is so important that we set out our understanding of performance.

Performance can be measured in a variety of ways, and there has been much dispute about what works for housing. The debate with the DoE (now the

DETR) and the Housing Corporation over statistical returns, with the Audit Commission over the Citizen's Charter measures, over what kind of measures are feasible for CCT specification and the emerging debate about *Best Value* illustrates the difficulties. Two main issues in the debate have been:

- how much can performance measures meet the requirement of measuring outcomes rather than inputs, e.g. resources or activities, i.e. the number of times a service is delivered;
- how much performance measures can be generalised at a national level, e.g. for use in league tables and how much they must be local and specific to have any managerial meaning.

However difficult it may prove, we would argue that the measuring, forecasting and monitoring must deal with four basic dimensions of performance (Holder, 1993).

Three relate directly to the service, namely:

- *quality or standard*, e.g. the customer satisfaction levels with repairs;
- *volume or amount*, e.g. the number of repair jobs;
- *cost*, e.g. the unit cost of repair jobs.

One relating directly to the effectiveness of the workforce, structure and systems, namely:

- *productivity* of the working organisation, e.g. the capacity of the maintenance section to turn repair jobs around.

Their connection is shown in a performance triangle – the direct service dimensions at the corners and productivity in the middle. The quality or standard of the service is the measure by which customers judge the service and they must have a close and real influence on the setting of, and maintenance of, standards.

**Figure 7.1: The four types of service performance**

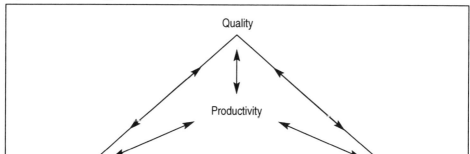

Housing organisations have often treated these four types separately, e.g. having quality improvement initiatives without considering the knock-on effects for costs, volume or productivity. Sustaining a business requires that this inter-relation be recognised. *Quality, volume and cost of services must be planned in conjunction with the organisation's productivity.* This is because:

- the current four performance levels represent the *current capacity of the organisation* to deliver a service;
- the four performance levels *must be in balance for the long-run survival of the business*;
- *if any one type of performance changes, there must be changes in one or more of the other three* – e.g. if quality must increase, volume will come down, costs will rise, or productivity will rise (or a combination of the three);
- *the capacity of the organisation to be more productive (e.g. preparing for CCT whilst running existing services) has its limits.* People become over stressed if workloads are not monitored and well enough managed over extended periods of time.

Sustaining your organisation's performance requires you to *measure, forecast and monitor* all four aspects of performance, *and* to assess the *knock-on effects* for the others if one has to change significantly We suggest you do this in the following way.

**Define the measures of quality, volume, cost and productivity**
Ensure you have key measures for performance for every aspect of your service. It is of course, a major piece of work to establish these measures systematically and a significant ongoing commitment to forecast and monitor them. However, housing organisations are increasingly recognising the benefits for sustaining their performance and using them for performance appraisal and business planning. Of the four measures types, quality and volume (or quantity), are now more readily available because of regulatory requirements by the DETR and the Housing Corporation. Costs, and particularly unit costs, are not so comprehensively available, but competitive pressures have, and we would argue, should, be forcing you to develop unit costs by type of service. Productivity is the measure of how much work a section is delivering. It will require the measurement of the time taken, volume of work, and numbers of people involved to calculate service volumes per staff member or team – a straightforward measure of productivity. This may seem a simplistic approach, but it is a start, and is increasingly seen as an organisational necessity. Better measures of performance can lead to improved performance, more effective allocation of staff resources and help avoid the 'burn-out' of individuals and teams through persistent overload. These benefits are beginning to be seen as well worth the costs of installing systematic time recording arrangements (whether full time or on a sampling basis) and evolving workload measurement systems to assess team and individual performance.

**Forecast performance**
Forecasting performance for ongoing services may mean little more than meeting well established quality, volume and cost targets. Meeting these targets requires staff and teams to be sustained and supported. If some targets are to be improved upon then the consequences for other targets must be considered. The days of unilaterally changing targets without working out the consequences, are over. If improvement in quality standards are required, will it mean less volume of service delivery? will costs be increased? will staff have to be more productive (perhaps through better IT equipment)? or, a combination of the three? Whatever is chosen, it is important to spell out the targets that cover all four dimensions.

**Monitor the results**
Regular, perhaps monthly, monitoring is increasingly the norm in housing organisations. This regular assessment of how well you are doing (or not), and taking action where necessary, is a key mechanism for sustaining your organisation's performance.

# People

The phrase "people are our most important resource", has been so often used by managers that its use can produce waves of cynicism within an organisation. Nonetheless, it is true. This section cannot cover the whole range of personnel or human resource policies; rather it makes a few points essential to sustaining the people of an organisation and therefore its business.

The first and most commonly missed point is that while all your attention and effort is on change, and on ensuring that those involved support the change, there are large numbers of staff continuing to deliver unchanging services. They need active support and recognition from managers, particularly senior managers, if the service is not to deteriorate through neglect.

One model that can be used for this purpose focuses upon ways in which staff commitment can be encouraged. Figure 7.2 (page 128) sets out the three 'pillars' that Peter Martin and John Nichols consider essential for this purpose (Martin and Nichols, 1987). They are:

- a sense of belonging to the organisation;
- excitement in the job;
- confidence in management leadership.

Whilst there are many models which cover this aspect of organisational life we believe this one is particularly helpful. Within the three pillars there are several facets, which can strengthen, or in their absence, weaken the commitment of staff.

**Figure 7.2: Gaining people's commitment to change**

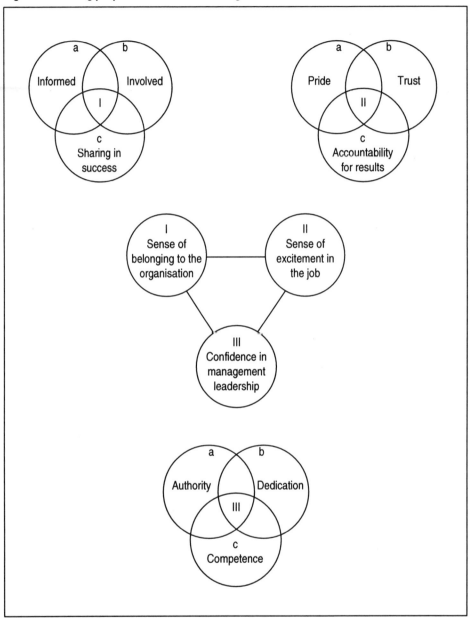

We would suggest you use the following checklist (Table 7.1). This checklist needs using for both staff going through change (which we cover in Chapter 9), and critically for those in the rest of the organisation. You need to question what you are doing on each (if anything), and ask if it adds up to a supportive, sustaining personnel strategy.

**Table 7.1: Creating commitment – pillars of commitment and their principal facets**

---

**Pillar 1: How to produce a sense of belonging to the organisation...**

*Inform people by:*
- team briefing
- open disclosure
- simple language and examples.

*Involve people by:*
- single status conditions
- consultation
- outings, visits and jamborees.

*Share success with people by:*
- celebrating achievements
- acknowledging good performance.

**Pillar 2: How to produce a sense of excitement in the job...**

*Create pride by:*
- responsibility for quality
- direct identification with output
- comparison with competitors.

*Create trust by:*
- clear delegation
- peer group control
- removal of demarcation.

*Create accountability for results by:*
- pushing decision-making down the line
- providing challenging tasks to achieve Best Value
- quality circles.

**Pillar 3: How to produce confidence in management leadership...**

*Exert authority by:*
- not allowing abdication of responsibility
- willingness to discipline
- maintaining of standards and objectives.

*Show dedication by:*
- reduction of management overheads
- seeking productivity through people
- attention to commitment.

*Display competence by:*
- establishing mission and objectives
- new management initiatives
- professional standards.

---

(Adapted from Martin and Nichols, op. cit.)

Looking down this list and the examples it will be clear that this sense of belonging, excitement and confidence is not merely a matter of checklist management. Rather it is important for the manager considers what range of measures are appropriate to their organisation, *and* taken together, will create a climate which builds each of these three aspects in a mutually supportive way. Several graphic examples of building commitment in this way have come from housing departments preparing for CCT in housing management. CCT has produced one of the biggest changes to local authority housing in recent years, and has forced managers to examine not only how they get staff to change but how they sustain everyone through the process and sustain the ongoing service delivery.

One department provides an example of dealing with all three *pillars*:

- For the first time it has instituted team briefing, it is consulting staff more fully than ever before, and with its regular reviews ensures that successes are celebrated – all contributing to a stronger sense of *belonging*.
- Key parts of the changes have included the identification of good practice and good quality work, engendering pride in the ongoing work of the department, increased delegation and trust has happened as senior managers have had their hands full with major changes, and alongside that has been the clear accountability for results (which have become easier to measure, if not to meet, with the specification of services) – contributing to a sense of *excitement* in the job.
- In the third area, leadership has been demonstrated through managers exercising their authority and making hard decisions, showing dedication and working long hours in preparation for CCT, and displaying competences which, despite many shaky moments, have seen the department through novel situations (e.g. preparing and running to business plans) – all building *confidence* in the management leadership.

It is not perfect, but the process substantially increased staff's commitment.

## An organisational sustaining audit

We have suggested in this chapter that you need to be active in maintaining and sustaining your organisation's performance. The chapter has set out a range of factors which it may be crucial for you to consider, analyse and take management action. We suggest that one way of pulling this together is to use the following list as the basis for a *sustaining audit* (Table 7.2). It is necessary to *assess* how much each question is relevant and what *action* might be taken.

The action will need to be integrated with your overall change planning (Chapter 9). There are two broad types of sustaining activity:

i.   Those which need dovetailing with activities central to the major changes you are undertaking, e.g. initiatives such as Investors in People or performance management, both of which will cover ongoing services as well as those undergoing change.

ii.  Those which are self standing but involve significant time and workload which will impact on the realism of the work commitments to changes being planned.

Both need clear thought, planned integration and joint monitoring to ensure effective overall management.

**Table 7.2: An organisational sustaining audit**

|  | Assessment | Action |
|---|---|---|
| **1. Purpose and Values**<br><br>*Purpose*<br><br>Is your organisational purpose clear, focused and operationalised through objectives or targets?<br><br>Is everyone aware of sticking to it?<br><br>*Values*<br><br>Which values require attention?<br><br>Are they clear, known by everyone, and 'owned' by the majority? |  |  |
| **2. Performance**<br><br>*Quality*<br><br>Do you have agreed measures?<br><br>Are you forecasting performance?<br><br>Do you regularly monitor results?<br><br>*Volume*<br><br>Do you have agreed measures?<br><br>Are you forecasting performance?<br><br>Do you regularly monitor results? |  | → |

| | Assessment | Action |
|---|---|---|
| *Cost* | | |
| Do you have agreed measures? | | |
| Are you forecasting performance? | | |
| Do you regularly monitor results? | | |
| *Productivity* | | |
| Do you have agreed measures? | | |
| Are you forecasting performance? | | |
| Do you regularly monitor results? | | |
| *Interconnection* | | |
| Are changes in one of the four aspects automatically considered for their knock-on effects on the others? | | |
| **3. People** | | |
| *Belonging* | | |
| How well are people informed? | | |
| How well are people involved? | | |
| How do they share success? | | |
| Is this resulting in an increased sense of belonging? | | |
| *Excitement* | | |
| How well is a sense of pride created? | | |
| How well is trust created? | | |
| How effectively are people held accountable for their results? | | |
| Is this resulting in a increased sense of excitement? | | → |

|  | Assessment | Action |
|---|---|---|
| *Leadership*<br><br>How well is authority exerted?<br><br>How is dedication shown?<br><br>How is competence demonstrated?<br><br>Is this resulting in a more credible leadership? |  |  |

# Further reading

Holder, A. (1993) *Business Planning,* Module 15 in *Competition and Local Authority Housing Services – A Guidance Manual*, Association of District Councils/Chartered Institute of Housing.

Kantor, R.M. et al. (1992) *The Challenge of Organisational Change*, The Free Press, New York.

Martin, P. and Nichols, J. (1987) *Creating a Committed Workforce*, Institute of Personnel Management, London.

Morgan, G. (1986) *Images of Organisations*, Sage, London.

# CHAPTER 8:
# What specifically needs to change and what needs sustaining?

**Objectives**
This chapter will enable you to:

- draw together your analysis based upon the work of the previous chapters;
- define what specifically should change;
- define what specifically should be sustained;
- draw upon the experience of two organisations that went through the process.

This will lead into the final chapters about implementing and leading the change.

## Introduction

A criticism often levelled at books written about managing change is that they encourage both too many new techniques, following the 'flavour of the month', and too much analysis, leading to the oft quoted sickness of 'paralysis by analysis'. We trust you will feel this book minimises both. Analysis must lead to appropriate action, not the panic reactions of 'we've got to do something' or 'we've got to do everything'. Analysis of the kind set out in the previous chapters has one aim – *to enable action to be taken that is appropriate to your situation.*

The book has been structured around the framework introduced in the first chapter and repeatedly referred to at the head of each chapter (Fig 8.1). Chapters 2 to 6 have set out in detail how various aspects of the change can be analysed in your organisation. Chapter 7 introduced the necessary and parallel analysis of what to sustain in your organisation. This leaves the two circles at the bottom left and right of the framework, *specific change* and *specific sustaining*. They are the subject of this chapter and their function is to draw together, as clearly as possible, your agenda for action. This provides a necessary discipline before moving onto the final two aspects of the change framework, *Getting from here to there* and *Where am I in all this?*, which follow in Chapters 9 and 10.

In this chapter we suggest how you might draw together your work from the

**Figure 8.1: A framework for organisation change**

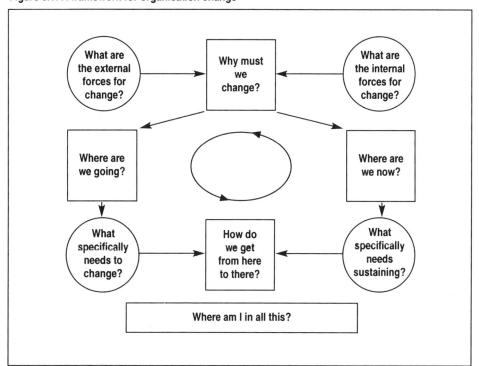

previous chapters. We do this by providing a checklist of key questions that relate to the framework for change. This is then illustrated by two examples; one a local authority housing department who were facing the competition of CCT, and one a housing association who were re-directing their business.

We would suggest a useful vehicle for drawing together your analysis is the production of a state-of-play report structured around the checklist of this chapter. It will draw together the various analyses, position papers, reports and ideas at a particular time and will reflect all the strengths and weaknesses of where you are at that point. Nonetheless the discipline focuses your agenda in a way which will greatly help your task of planning and implementing change.

# Specific changes and specific sustaining

This section should to draw together the work from the previous chapters.

### External forces for change (Chapter 2)

External forces can be reduced to four key questions:

- What changes in the economy will affect you?
- How will demographic and social change impact on you?
- What are current and future government policies likely to mean for you?
- What are the key local influences to which you will have, or want, to respond?

These may have been drawn together in your PEST Analysis (Political, Economic, Social and Technological forces).

### Internal forces for change (Chapter 3)

Considering internal forces requires seven key questions to be asked:

- What changes does the SWOT analysis suggest are necessary?
- How strong is the political or managerial leadership?
- Are there, or have there been, key decisions about the organisation's future?
- How supportive of change is the organisation's culture?
- How much planning for change has there been?
- How much room is there to improve efficiency and effectiveness?
- What obstacles are there to effective organisational functioning – to being fit for purpose?

With both external and internal forces there is a need to be clear about the *likely impact* they will have on your organisation, *the degree of certainty /uncertainty* that it will have this impact, and *what alternatives* are likely.

### Why must we change? (Chapter 4)

This analysis should have led to clarification of the key factors:

- What are the triggers for change? Are they still valid and sufficient reason for change?
- What are the relevant factors and techniques of analysis? What are the conclusions and consequences?
- What commitments are there likely to be from key stakeholders to support the changes? Who will be driving the changes and who will be resisting them? What negotiations are necessary?

### Where are we now? (Chapter 5)

This question may have highlighted many issues but it is important to draw together the answers to two key questions from the capability assessment.

- What appears, or does not appear, to be working well?
- What changes might be made to improve the functioning of the organisation?

### Where are we going? (Chapter 6)

Your consideration of where you wish to go will be incomplete and inevitably be patchy first time but it should include consideration of the following questions:

- What options have you identified for dealing with the pressures for change?
- What guiding principles do you have for choosing between options?
- Have you considered the case for mission statements, aims and objectives?
- How will you measure the success of the change?

### What specifically needs sustaining? (Chapter 7)

The following key areas were drawn together in the organisational sustaining audit.

- Is your organisational *purpose* focused, widely shared and delivered through objectives or targets?
- Are your *values* clear, known by everyone, and 'owned' by the majority of staff?
- How well are the four aspects of ongoing service *performance* – quality, volume, cost and productivity – measured, forecast and monitored?
- To what extent do people feel a sense of belonging and excitement in your organisation and a trust in its management leadership?

## Changing and sustaining illustrated

In this section we illustrate how two organisations brought their thinking and analysis together. Both are amalgamations of several actual organisations and are therefore unidentified and we trust unidentifiable!

We have used the framework because it provides a structure for being systematic about the analysis of any organisational change and it is a useful way of summarising the key issues that need managing in change. We trust this will

enable you to pull together the agenda for action when you are making a major
change and are about to plan the detail of implementation.

## Case study A: preparing for competition and CCT

Local Authority A, with a 10,000 housing stock, had to prepare for CCT against
a two and a half year deadline. The authority is on the edge of a major
conurbation and has a wide social mix of population and typical demands on its
services. In recent years it had made a series of improvements to the service
which offered tenants a better maintenance service, clearer allocations criteria,
better customer care and, despite financial and stock constraints, an effective
homelessness service to the community. It had developed a close working
relationship – despite historic resistances at political and officer level – with
local housing associations, moving, for example towards a common housing
register. Finances were tight, practically non-existent on capital, and there were
increasing cross-authority effort being put into Single Regeneration bids and
European Union bids – taking increasing amounts of senior managers' time.

Recently there had been a change of director and two others at the senior
management team level. Turnover in the department as a whole was low because
of few job opportunities elsewhere and morale was stable though low because of
year on year financial cutbacks. Political direction was none too clear, though
with the continuity of a single party there was a degree of certainty about the
basic policies of, *'keeping the stock, minimising the impact of the cuts and keep
making improvements as we always have!'*.

Internally the department had begun to introduce service plans, a half way house
in name as well as substance to business plans, a name politicians would not
countenance. It was felt by senior managers that the department was moving
forward on the quality of its management and staffing by providing some
systematic training which tied into national standards and a newly introduced –
and therefore not quite established – staff appraisal and development scheme.
There was some scepticism amongst staff about whether the changes being
introduced and the CCT challenges being faced would make any difference to a
hard situation which is seen as yearly getting worse.

Three months into his new job the director initiated a thorough review of the
department's predicament as it faced a recently clarified CCT deadline. After a
further two months of specific analysis by the four assistant directors the
following results emerged:

### What are the external forces for change? (Chapter 2)
- Two year lead into CCT competition for Housing Management,
  requiring a specification, costing and assessment of the emerging
  competition.
- A likely 5 per cent real reduction in finance year on year.

- Continuing high local unemployment making housing revenue rent and housing benefit change sensitive.

## What are the internal forces for change? (Chapter 3)

- A new management team keen to strengthen a *customer first* culture and tackle long-run problems.
- Variation in standards, procedures and management, much not written down, which would need tackling for CCT and creation of *one service* across the department.
- Low morale and a common belief that *nothing could change; it never has!*
- IT was fitfully progressing through an over-stretched and under-budgeted IT/IS section.
- An ambitious human resource section which was *making waves* with its systematic training plans and new appraisal/development scheme which managers were finding very time consuming to implement.

## Why must we change? (Chapter 4)

The departmental management team undertook, as part of an 'Awayday', a Porter Five Box analysis of their situation. The results are similar to those summarised in Chapter 4, Figure 4.2. The management team drew a number of conclusions from this analysis which began to answer the question, *why must we change?* They were:

- The preparation and winning of the HMCCT contract would not be easy because of likely external competition and internal weaknesses. It would require a tough programme of action to get the Department ready.
- Currently there was *no direct competition* (Box A) – it was the early days of CCT – but the healthy competition for the council's maintenance contracts (several contracts had gone to outside contractors) demonstrated that the council was known as a significant source of 'good work'.
- At this stage their assessment of *new entrants* (Box B) was that the contract would be attractive to a range of likely competitive organisations from local LSVT associations wishing to expand, to local (not very credible), national and international facilities management companies. The range of interest was the product of the authority's prime geographical location which would provide a very accessible base for further CCT bids in the wider area. The cost, quality *and*, crucially, composition of the contract (including "non-defined parts difficult for the competition to handle) would all need to be employed.
- Other options to CCT – *substitute* services (Box C) – were very limited. Tenant managed organisations would have an equally tight

time scale even if the politicians were keen, which they weren't, and the right-to-buy figures would not realistically bring the figures to de minimus levels thereby missing CCT. Facing CCT was the most realistic option.

- Although a good deal more complicated than *buyers* in the normal market place (Box D), tenants would have to (because of the government's requirements) and should be (because of the council's extension of tenant participation), heavily involved in specifying and choosing levels of service for the contract.
- And finally, the *suppliers* (Box E),would be going through considerable change themselves, notably council services facing their own CCT pressures. The team felt that this would enable pressure to be exerted on central finance, personnel and law to get better and cheaper services (it was felt that the Housing Revenue Account had long been an 'easy touch' for central overheads). This would need careful handling as the other services had a less tight deadline and could just 'dig in their heals'.

The upshot of this analysis was that CCT would clearly have to be faced. It would be very demanding as continued service delivery was hard enough, and it would require preparation on a wide number of fronts, notably specifying, agreeing and delivering consistent service quality, working to much tighter costs, and understanding the nature of the competition as it emerged.

**Where are we now? (Chapter 5)**
One of the assistant directors undertook a rapid and, as it proved, highly effective 'health check' to assess what aspects of the department would need to change and what needed sustaining. Techniques used were a selection, and in most cases a simplification, of those set out in Chapter 6. They were:

- A *values exercise* which distilled the values a cross-section of staff thought important. This list of values was reduced to a core set and then tested in the rest of the department. Once a measure of agreement had been reached the values statement was made a requirement of all teams, each being required to set targets as to how they would change over the next six months.
- A *SWOT analysis* emerged from a selection of groups across the department identifying a range of strengths to build on and weaknesses to tackle. It demonstrated wide agreement that the department was strong on committed, able, knowledgeable staff and weak on procedures and systems that worked sensibly and consistently. In addition, cost awareness was low, different estates were highly competitive and didn't support one another, everyone had feelings of being under huge pressure.
- A *profiling of current service delivery* took place to establish;
    - what policies and standards were available to staff;

- what were actively being worked to;
- what performance data was available and what it showed was actually delivered;
- what time recording data was available (which could begin to define costs).

Inevitably this revealed a range of gaps and inconsistencies in policies and standards and many differences between policy and practice. The full extent of the changes necessary would need further work and certainly phasing over the CCT preparation period.

- An *outline health check* by the management team of the department's structures, systems, skills and culture, the key question being were they fit for the forthcoming challenge of CCT? This produced a long list of reshaping ideas which had to be put together with other material and initial priorities established.

### Where are we going? (Chapter 6)

It was clear from even this initial analysis that the department would have to respond to the forces it faced; staying as it was, was not an option. However, at this stage there was no detailed assessment of future options as spelt out in Chapter 6. Many ideas were brought together, some were from within the department and arose from 'solutions' to current problems, others were from external sources, e.g. how other authorities were tackling the preparation for CCT, cultural change and business planning. Rather than let these ideas evaporate they were put into a 'Possibilities Paper' and were used and tested at later and more appropriate stages.

### Being specific

At this stage the department decided to take the following steps for changing and sustaining its activities.

### What specifically needed sustaining? (Chapter 7)

- Encourage teams to be clear what they regard as strengths which they must sustain.
- Utilise key skills in drawing up the specification.

### What specifically needed to change? (Chapter 8)

At this stage the department decided to make the following specific changes:

- Document and rationalise service policies, standards and procedures
- Review, with staff, realistic changes in service delivery consistent with standards.
- Train staff in new CCT ways of working.
- Introduce a system of regular two-way team briefing to strengthen communications.
- Identify and carry through phased improvements to financial, management and information systems.
- Monitor and develop a database about local and national competition.

**Pulling it together**

This sketch of the 'Director's review', which took place over a two month period, shows only the bare bones of the analysis and conclusions. What the review did was to signal to everyone in the department that the management team were taking the challenge seriously, they were not doing it on their own; and they were speedy but thorough in their approach, using a variety of techniques. Despite claims that a series of management team 'Awaydays' to pull the material together were 'management jaunts', the emerging action plan for the next six months (with a sketchier two year outline) was soon felt to have real consequences and really work! This initial assessment of the changes which needed to prepare for CCT did much to provide clear leadership in uncertain times. Whilst much had to be reassessed as the situation changed and later became clearer, the breadth and seriousness of this review provided a base which reassured both managers and staff. It also fostered something new in the department, a commitment to deliver action plans once they were agreed.

## Case study B: extending a housing association's role

Housing association B had extended its stock to 2,200 properties and had reached a plateau. Larger, nationally operating associations were able to outbid the association in local developments. The local authorities who were familiar with the association's reputation were nonetheless tempted by the inducements that the bigger associations were offering. There were also numerous smaller associations which were sometimes co-operative and sometimes competitive. The Association was uncertain of its role and relationships, particularly with the local authorities.

The association under an 'ever restless' chief executive had made big strides with its internal management and organisation. But the development division having been the leading edge had begun to have fewer 'successes' and was losing its way. Management had, however, begun to develop its practice both in quality and consistency and tenants were generally very satisfied with the management of their homes. The chief executive and management team decided they must find a way of being clear about its strategic future. Here is what they discovered in their analysis.

**What are the external forces for change? (Chapter 2)**
- The grant rate falling year on year was making the development department's bids less competitive or more financially risky.
- Relationships with local authorities were becoming less secure.
- Several overtures were being made to the Association to manage stock for other associations and the MoD; amalgamate with other smaller associations; and offer other services to smaller association such as legal, maintenance and building materials supplies.

**What are the internal forces for change? (Chapter 3)**

- A new chairman of the management committee was wanting a more clearly stated and agreed strategy.
- Members of the management team were keen to meet the challenge of external change proactively.
- A range of staff were particularly talented and showed signs of restlessness because the association gave no consistent signal of expanding its role and thereby offering challenges and excitement to them.
- All these three elements came together, not in an environment of having 'nothing to do', rather the reverse. Each demonstrated that whilst there was much to do in keeping the service delivery going and attending to deficiencies there had to be new challenges.

**Why must we change? (Chapter 4)**

The association's management team decided to organise a facilitated, two day workshop, away from the office. Its purpose was to analyse the forces for change, establish criteria for judging the options and generate as many realistic options as possible. From this, a new strategy, or strategic options, could be shaped up to meet the forces for change whilst sustaining current service strengths – a strategy for development.

The team undertook several pieces of analysis:

- *A SWOT analysis*, particularly to identify where 'movement' was either essential or opportunistic.
- Out of this came a need to *examine internal problems* which needed resolving. It would be over-stating the case to say that Ohmae's technique was used as set out in Chapter 4, but the same type of radical thinking led to some key arguments for change. Several of them centred around the case for establishing a better critical mass of a service in order to develop economies of scale – a problem affecting several aspects of the association's direct and indirect services.
- Equally the *analysis of external forces*, whilst not a thorough going Porter analysis, did examine the case for expansion in the size of operation and diversification of services offered.
- The upshot of this was the identification of *four areas of potential development* – a four leaf clover shape which was used throughout the workshop from then on. The areas of extension were:
  - *housing management services* through CCT bids and acting as management agents to other associations and private landlords;
  - *housing stock* by merger or stock transfer;
  - *the range of direct housing services* to single young persons/elderly persons not currently offered;
  - *the range of indirect products and services* from component manufacture to legal services.

**Where are we now? (Chapter 5)**

The workshop had started with a SWOT analysis which identified many aspects of the association's current strengths and weaknesses. The future options which had been generated highlighted parts of the organisation that would need to undergo change. Whilst the workshop did not have time to do a detailed assessment of the current position it did identify follow-up work that was necessary to clarify the basis for change, namely, work on the values, aims and objectives for services, and on staff attitudes and skills.

**Where are we going? (Chapter 6)**

Before undertaking detailed work on the four areas of potential development, the criteria for judging the options was established. This emerged as a set of criteria against five headings, namely the benefits for:

- Tenants, e.g. to give them real choices about services and maintenance.
- The Association, e.g. to survive and satisfy funders.
- Local authorities, e.g. to be sensitive to their particular needs.
- The Housing Corporation, e.g. to meet their narrow value for money criteria without compromising financial viability.
- Staff, e.g. to provide personal development opportunities through comprehensive training.

These were used not just to assess the final options but to shape the options as they emerged.

The team then divided into two groupings which took first one and then another opportunity area – thus covering all four – and were asked to generate realistic options in each area. The detail is both unnecessary and too confidential to give here but a common form of analysis was used. Each idea was subjected to the following tests:

- What are the benefits?
- What are the costs?
- Forces for change
- Forces against change
- What action should be taken?

Tests three and four were part of a force field analysis which we have discovered many managers find useful in assessing the realism of change (Chapter 9). Each group presented its findings at each stage and it was subjected to a rigorous critique by the other group. The overall results were put together identifying the 'clover leaf' pattern of options.

**What specifically needed sustaining? (Chapter 7)**

Part of the follow-up work to the workshop was to check out the values that the association should hold to, the aims and objectives that needed changing, those that needed sustaining, and to assess whether the attitudes and skills of staff were appropriate, or not, to the proposed changes.

**What specifically needed to change? (Chapter 8)**
A clear list of options had been developed during the workshop and the way in which they would be investigated. This list after further testing, debate and discussion with the management committee formed the basis of a strategy document that has been used during the past few years to extend the association's activities.

**Pulling it together**
This brief workshop by one association demonstrates the value and progress that can be made in a relatively short space of time. It greatly helped this team to 'picture' the options available to it and to plan a way of establishing a realistic and worked through strategy. As the chief executive said in the succeeding months, "it was the easy part," progressing it and getting it carried through proved difficult despite good will. Other pressures of the day-to-day nature repeatedly got in the way. It is now well established and being used to direct the Association, not slavishly, but providing a guide which all staff are aware of.

# In conclusion

We trust you have found your way through the analyses and frameworks here. They are intended as aids for pulling your assessment together – taking stock before the next stage of planning the implementation. If the techniques get in the way don't use them. What is most important is that you are convinced that your analysis and proposed actions are appropriate to the demands of the situation. Whilst the court room requirement of, 'beyond all reasonable doubt' may be a little too demanding a test for your proposals, then at least let your 'doubts be reasonable'.

# CHAPTER 9:
# How do we get from here to there?

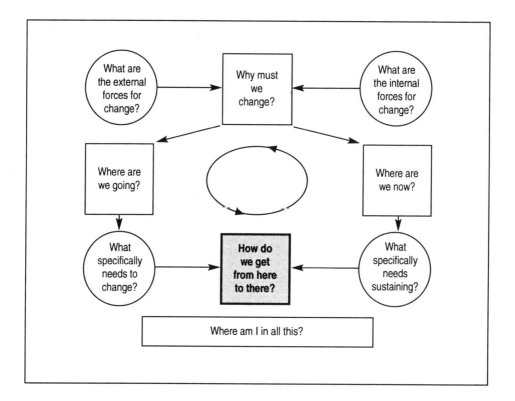

**Objectives:**
This chapter will enable you to:

- identify and critically assess all the factors helping and hindering a specific change, and be able to plan an agenda of actions needed to progress it.
- understand how individuals react to change and have some strategies to assist them to deal with it;
- have a range of tools, techniques and strategies that can be drawn upon, as appropriate, to progress specific organisational changes.

# Introduction

Chapter 5 explored and suggested practical ways of establishing and understanding the current state of the organisation, and Chapter 6 took you through the process of forming a clear picture of where you want the organisation to be. It is only after you have completed these two process can you start to consider how you are going to achieve your goals.

This chapter concerns itself with the mechanics of moving the organisation from where it is at present to where you want it to be. It offers some useful concepts concerning change management as well as some tools and techniques helpful to individuals leading or involved in the change. Although the emphasis in the book so far is on wide scale strategic change, most of the techniques and and methods outlined in this chapter are just as relevant to managers introducing or implementing smaller scale changes. Indeed this chapter is concerned with the more practical issue of how managers can implement changes. Where we refer to the organisation, readers can substitute department, section or team, although, of course, we need to be aware of the effect any changes in department, section or team practice, performance or behaviour will have on the wider organisation and customers.

Leading change in organisations is not a simple and straightforward process. There are no hard and fast rules for managing change successfully. Every organisation will have different issues to resolve, different cultures and traditions to work with, and different individuals with different skills. It is up to the leaders of the change to choose a path which is best suited for their specific organisations and circumstances. There are however a number of factors that need to be considered and addressed in any change. The depth and level at which those factors are considered will depend on whether the change is strategic or operational (see Chapter 1).

These can be classified generally into two.

a) The systems, techniques and ways of organising, i.e. the **mechanics of change** which include:
   - Assessing the overall change agenda (see previous chapters).
   - Establishing a compelling reason to change (see Chapter 4).
   - Assessing the current health of the organisation (see Chapter 5).
   - Sustaining the ongoing work of the organisation during the change process (see Chapter 7).
   - Planning, preparing and timing changes.
   - Getting started and progressing change by using change agents.
   - Watching for the changing agenda, and adapting to changing circumstances.

b) The issues, concerns of individuals and how to **take people with you** which include:
- Individuals' need to know and what the implications are for them.
- Individual reactions to change and need for support.
- Communication processes during change, distinguishing between informing, involving and delegating.
- Team establishment and development.
- Training and development in new roles, relationships and ways of working.
- Training and informing individuals and teams about specific changes in systems and processes.

This chapter will first look at the mechanics of managing change, offering some tools, techniques and guidelines for getting the change process started and progressed. The second half of the chapter will explore some of the issues around people and change; how people react to change and what can be done by managers and leaders of change to take people with them.

# Mechanics of change

## *Where to start*

Deciding on where to begin in any change programme often presents the manager with an overwhelming array of things to do and anticipated blockages to achieving the end result. One technique that is useful at this stage is a *force field analysis*. This is not a complicated scientific process, it is very simply a method of deepening your understanding of the current situation, and identifying the most appropriate place to start on the change process and the formulation of an action plan.

**Figure 9.1: Force field analysis**

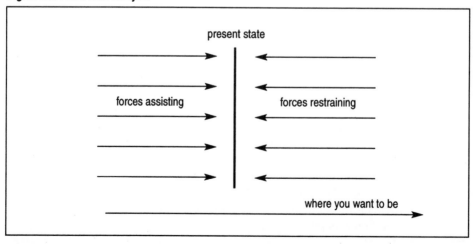

The diagram above illustrates the basis of the analysis. It starts from the idea that the present situation represents an equilibrium between forces driving change and forces resisting change, which are in tension, i.e. a force field. The identification of those forces, their direction, nature, strength and how they can be modified is the 'force field analysis'.

There are a number of stages to the process:

1.  Make a clear statement about where you want to be or your outcome.

2.  Identify and list all those elements that are:
    a)  driving forces, and
    b)  restraining forces.
    These forces are likely to include: personal; interpersonal, group; inter-group, cultural, administrative, technological, environmental (make sure you include yourself!).

3.  Analyse each of the forces. How influential/strong are they and have you any control over them? What are the connections between the forces, e.g. if you influenced one would it affect another?

4.  Rank those that you can influence in order of importance.

5.  Identify practical actions that you could take which will:
    *   build on the driving forces;
    *   reduce the resisting forces.
    It is important to note that building the driving forces alone will generally have the effect of increasing the resisting forces. A classic example of this is increasing management force in an industrial dispute will normally have the effect of increasing union/staff resistance!
    At this stage it is often the case that managers discover that the outcome identified at the beginning is too large-scale and complex to deal with in one analysis and that individual 'forces' have their own force fields to be identified.

6.  Develop a detailed action plan with target dates. Remembering that making small steps on a number of fronts is usually more effective in the long-run than trying to achieve too much in a short space of time.

Force field analysis can be used in a variety of situations, from large-scale organisational change to personal career planning. It is a very effective tool to use with groups, who often find it helps them picture 'the whole' of a problem and enables them to be creative about solutions.

Next we present a real example of how force field analysis was used to assist a new training manager in a housing department of a large local authority, to begin the task of developing and implementing a training strategy. This was her first attempt, it did not cover all the issues, since new ones cropped up as she progressed with her initiative. The value of it was, that it helped her to put down all her ideas and thoughts in one picture of the situation, made her think more clearly about the elements at play, and helped her decide on the most appropriate place to begin.

She was able to use the force field at various stages of the process, reworking the forces as they changed and developed. It was particularly useful, at points where she felt stuck, helping her to see a way forward.

**Exercise**
Use the force field framework to analyse an issue or project which you are currently working on and having difficulty progressing.

---

## Example 9.1: Force Field Analysis

**Summary of current situation**
New training manager, large London borough housing department, no current training strategy. Majority of budget being spent on professional qualification courses, little in-house training, no systematic or fair way of allocating resources. Training initiatives that do exist, are implemented in a haphazard way, effectiveness of training not measured. Training generally not well regarded in department although the need is recognised by a significant number of staff and managers.

**Stage 1. Where you want to be**
A developed and implemented training strategy, putting more resources into in-house training, reducing amount spent on qualification courses, making training more responsive to needs of service and in line with equal opportunities good practice.

**Stage 2. Identify driving and restraining forces**
(include personal, interpersonal, group, inter-group, administrative, technological, environmental and yourself!)

| DRIVING → | ← RESTRAINING |
|---|---|
| My energy | Current students |
| Equal opportunities principles and lobby union on behalf of current and potential students | Career structures in professional areas such as surveying |
| Staff not currently getting training | |
| Group of interested managers | No procedures |
| Union wanting more training | Low training budget |
| Management team | Very limited staffing resources |

---

**Stage 3. Analyse each of the forces**
(How important are they? Have you any control over them? What are the connections between them? If you influence one will it affect another?)

1. **Management team** – influence, important.

2. **My energy** – important to keep up.

3. **Equal opportunities** – principles important, individuals not so influential.

4. **Staff** – unlikely to be a power base. Union will take up issues.

5. **Interested managers** – important, need them for implementation.

6. **Union** – weak base, influences staff for and against, I have some influence.

7. **Current students** – will lobby, will use union.

8. **Career structures dependent on acquisition of qualifications.**

9. **Procedures** – important, without cannot implement.

10. **Low training budget.**

**Stage 4. Rank those forces you can influence in order of importance**

1. Procedures and systems:

2. Management team, and interested managers:

3. Develop strategy (using managers and management team as sounding boards):

4. Unions:

5. Current students:

6. My energy:

7. Disinterested managers and staff – take some time to win them over:

→

**Stage 5. Identify actions *you* can take to:**
a) *build on driving forces*
- Keep training on agenda of management team, form training panel of managers to find out training needs and involve in strategy formulation.
- Find support for me and a sounding board for ideas.
- Use equal opportunities arguments and ensure principles are adhered to in all strategy and procedures.
- Speak independently to at least two members of management team, persuade them to advocate on behalf of training

b) *reduce the restraining/resisting forces*
- Design system for recording and monitoring current and future training activities, use figures in arguments.
- Develop strategy in consultation with senior managers set time limits for its approval at committee.
- Begin dialogue with union on strategy development, use equal opportunities arguments, show more training and development will be given to more staff, strategy will develop each year.
- Publicise benefits of new approach throughout department.

**Stage 6. List actions that you need to take with target dates**
(remember the smaller the action the more likely it is to be achieved)

| Action | Target date |
| --- | --- |
| *Agree terms reference and set up training panel* | *One month from today* |
| *Ask to have regular monthly report to management team* | *Tomorrow* |
| *Draft new training strategy for first meeting of panel* | *Six weeks* |
| *Ring colleague in another borough to test out ideas* | *One week* |

## Identifying the stakeholders

A key aspect of any change situation or problem to be managed is the accurate identification of the individuals or groups who have a stake in either the future being planned or keeping the current status quo, in other words, the stakeholders. A full discussion of the role of stakeholders in the strategic planning process is in Chapter 4, p.64. It is clear from this, that stakeholders play a key role throughout the change process and that energy has to be put into ensuring they play a relevant role. If this is not done there is a high chance that they will affect the change either adversely or in a way which is unplanned and uncontrolled. Stakeholders may be inside or outside the organisation, may be individuals, groups or institutions.

A simple diagram can help you note who the stakeholders are, and their relationships to each other and the change.

**Figure 9.1: Identifying stakeholders and their interests**

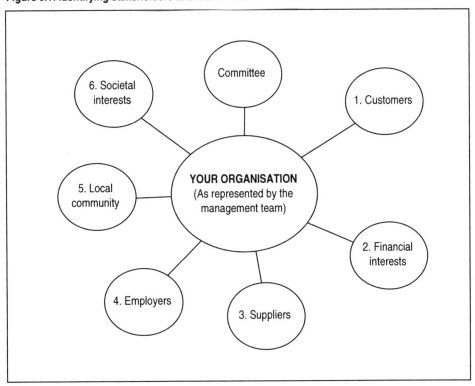

Having identified the stakeholders, the next step is to examine their relationship to the change.

Questions to ask include:

- What are their interests in the change?
- What power do they have to facilitate or resist the change?
- What decisions or actions are needed from them, and when?
- What current aspects of the relationship need to be fostered and or changed?
- What type and nature of relationships do you need to foster with them for the future?

Once the above analysis has been done, you are then in a position to identify what actions you and others need to take to keep the stakeholders 'on board'. Consideration should be given to:

- What level of involvement each of them requires.
- How, when and how frequently you need to involve each of them.

- Is there a significant or more effective sequence you will need to use when involving them, e.g. will one stakeholder only 'come on board' if another is already there?
- Who are the most appropriate individuals or groups to do the liaising effectively (this may well not be you!).

The stakeholder 'analysis' needs to be revisited at various stages during the change process to check whether it is still an accurate picture. New stakeholders may come into the frame, they need to be considered similarly, also stakeholders identified at the beginning of the process may lose their significance for one reason or another.

Stakeholder analysis is a useful tool to use with a management or task group initiating and managing a change. Doing it in a group increases the chances of compiling a more comprehensive picture as well as allowing views and ideas to come forward regarding the best 'tactics'. This in turn increases the understanding of those in the group of what is involved and the actions which need to be taken.

## Getting things moving: the role of change agents

If any change is to be successful the process needs to be led and facilitated by one or more individuals. These individuals have to be internal to the organisation. Even where external consultants are used to 'introduce change' their success will be dependent on the extent to which there is ownership of the change within the organisation.

At the beginning of any change process, ownership usually rests with a few individuals. These individuals must become the change agents, facilitating and moving the change forward. It is also important to remember that even if you have conceived a change or a change is your particular responsibility, you may not be the most appropriate person to take the leading role in that change. However appealing and exciting it may seem, you must ask yourself whether you are the best choice to take the lead. The larger the change the more change agents are needed, these need not necessarily be senior managers, change agents can be recruited from across the organisation.

Key features of change agents are that they must:

- **be in favour of the change**. This seems to be an obvious statement, however many change initiatives have failed due to the fact that the individual 'in charge' is there by virtue of their position in the organisation and not their commitment to change. There are, of course occasions where we have to implement something we do not entirely agree with. In these cases it is important that we make sense of the change for ourselves, and find some positive value in the change. If we fail to do this, people will not be convinced and are unlikely to work alongside us. Eventually we are unable to sustain the energy to carry it through. Chapter 4 explores further the issue of 'Why Change'.

- **be respected by staff**. This does not necessarily mean the most popular person or someone who has the most senior position. Change agents may be respected for different things. It is important to identify the qualities that will be important to gain the respect of everyone involved in the change process, e.g. technical expertise, independence, a previous known success, good organisational skills, good communication skills etc.
- **be able to influence others**. However good someone is technically, if they have not got the ability influence others the change project will run into difficulties.

Whoever the change agents are, there are a number of rules of thumb that they should bear in mind:

1. **Stay alive**; don't become so involved with change problems that you sacrifice yourself in an attempt to solve them. You need to remember, not all problems can be solved nor are they your sole responsibility. You need to recognise the difference between the 'intervention failed' and 'I failed'.

2. **Start where the system is**; get a clear picture of what the current state of the organisation is, and start from that point. This includes not only systems and procedures but also the culture of the organisation (the way things are done) and of course the feelings and thoughts of the individuals involved in the change (see Chapter 5).

3. **Never work uphill**; *don't build hills as you go* – avoid activities that have a positive impact on one group and a negative impact on others, e.g. beginning a customer care strategy by training front-line staff in customer care, when middle and senior managers are unable to deal with the issues arising due to their lack of training and preparation. Work *in the most promising arenas* – choose an area to start where there is a high chance of success.
*Build resources*, don't attempt to do it alone, use others' energy, enthusiasm, skills, influence and creativity. *Don't over-organise* or get locked into a plan, going with the flow is important on occasion. *Don't argue if you can't win*. Don't make enemies, winning the battle may lose you the war. *Play God but just a little*. You will need to make value judgements at times, if you don't someone else will. Be in touch with your values and stick with them.

4. **Innovation needs a good idea, initiative and friends**; have a sounding board to help maintain perspective and purpose.

5. **Light lots of fires**; start in a number of different places, change will get talked about and spread easier. If one 'fire' goes out others will still be alight.

6. **Keep an optimistic bias**; interventions are weakened by those who are pessimistic about outcomes.

7. **Capture the moment**; relevance and timing are crucial in implementing change, sometimes it is good to go with the 'feels right' rather than waiting for everything to be perfect before moving forward.

8. **You will make mistakes**; learn from mistakes, move forward and do not make them excuses for stopping.

### The role of external consultants in organisational change

There has been a tremendous growth in the use of external consultants by housing organisations in the last few years. There are some obvious reasons for this. Large-scale changes such as CCT, LSVT, mergers, takeovers, formation of housing companies have been experiences which our industry have not faced before. These changes have often been done within tight time scales. Many organisations have had to ask themselves whether they have the specialist skills, time resource or confidence to undertake many of the activities necessary for successful transition and have used external consultants to fill these gaps.

The many different types of role external consultants can fulfil fall into two main categories. Firstly, those dealing with the technical aspects of a change, e.g. putting in a particular IT system, conducting a financial appraisal, undertaking a stock condition survey. Secondly, those concerned with helping organisations deal with the process of change which are more to do with assisting people through the changes. These roles include: mentoring managers, supporting in-house teams leading or implementing changes, counselling individuals facing decisions about their futures in the organisation.

Independence is fundamental to whatever role a consultant fulfils. Consultants can provide that crucial independent view of the organisation, not affected by the histories and feelings which often colour the views of people within it. It is often said a consultant's report will have greater credibility than an internally generated report (even though they may have come to exactly the same conclusion). In assisting organisations in the process of change, independence is valuable, particularly in the areas of mentoring individuals or supporting teams. However, where staff or others involved in the change feel that consultants are not independent they can be the focus of any anger or frustration within the organisation and reinforce negative feelings about senior managers and the organisation. We have talked at length in this book about the importance of people within the organisation owning change, therefore care needs to be taken when employing consultants that attention is given to nurturing this ownership and not as can easily happen, that ownership be transferred or attributed to the consultant(s).

When making a decision about whether to use external consultants it is important to be clear about why they are being employed and the role they are to undertake. Questions to ask include:

- Do we have the skills and resources in-house?
- Do we need the independence?
- What will their role be?
- Are we clear about the task or do we need help to define it?
- How will we maintain ownership of the change?
- What will happen at the end of the contract?

This last question is important. Any organisation using a consultant should think about their dependency on that consultant. All consultants assisting organisations in change should be concerned with helping the organisation to function more effectively after their intervention and should be asked in detail about how they will work towards this, before any contract is agreed.

## Scheduling the change

Trying to keep track of complex change can be likened to a juggling act, keeping your eyes on the balls, dealing with the ones flying in from the sides without dropping any, and all the while keeping smiling!

One mechanism which is extremely useful for scheduling the change is the Gantt chart. It may not help you maintain the smile but it will provide a complete view of what should happen and when. The Gantt chart is a method of identifying tasks and activities which need to be done, against a time scale. In its simplest form it can be drawn roughly on a flip chart to give an overview of the change process. This is an extremely good way for groups involved in planning or implementing change to get an overall view of what is to be done. Individuals in the group can then contribute ideas and information to enhance the picture, spotting possible problem areas, work overloads, etc. (Figure 9.2 illustrates a personnel section's use of it).

**Figure 9.2: One group's simple chart for a change in a recruitment procedure**

|  | March | April | May | June |
|---|---|---|---|---|
| Training |  | ************** |  |  |
| Publicity |  |  | *********** |  |
| Procedure note |  | ******* | ***** |  |
| Troubleshoot |  |  |  | **** |
| Going live |  |  |  | * |

The original plan for this personnel section, who were introducing a significant change in the recruitment procedures for their organisation, allowed four weeks to write the procedure which would be added to the personnel procedure manual prior to training all managers involved in recruitment and selection. However they amended their plan after putting together the simple chart above. In discussing the chart, the group identified that there might be a need for procedure notes to be amended as a result of training sessions, and only after this, could the detail be publicised and put in the manual. In thinking it through, they also realised that there may well be issues arising from the change once it had gone 'live', therefore resources would be needed for trouble shooting in the period following going live.

There are computer programs available commercially, which offer frameworks to plot, plan and progress complex change. These techniques have been around for a long time and used in many areas of housing, e.g. in development work. In our work with managers in housing we have noticed that although techniques may be helpful and used in specific areas they are, as a general rule, unfortunately not translated or transferred for use in other areas or on different types of issues.

# Taking people with you

## *Resistance to change*

Resistance is: *Any conduct that tries to maintain the status quo in the face of pressure to change.*

Any manager trying to introduce a change will recognise this definition and no doubt be able to produce a long list of behaviours falling into this category. The list would probably include, procrastination in decision-making, finding urgent tasks to do rather than progress change, phrases like 'we've tried that before and it didn't work', increase in sickness levels, consultation processes that replace action, etc.

So why do people resist change?

- A desire not to lose something of value.
- Historical factors – how previous changes have been handled.
- Misunderstanding of change and its implicàtions.
- Uncertainty about how much freedom there is to do things differently.
- Lack of skills in decision-making or experience of implementing change.
- Existing commitments, social and psychological to present services.
- Fear of uncertainty and complexity.

- Management want change therefore staff resist it.
- How the change is being handled.
- Changitis! (weariness with constant and rapid change).

The above list is not exhaustive but it does cover a wide range of the common reasons for resistance. It is a useful list in that it does identify some of the pitfalls managers fall into when introducing change. And it usefully provides a list of changes which may personally affect the manager or change agent.

It is important not only to recognise these behaviours and the possible reasons for them, but also to understand and predict them. Leaders of change can then develop strategies to work with people to overcome the resistance, and encourage more positive behaviours.

One classic illustration of resistance to change involved a new chief executive in a local authority who introduced a new information system into his department, within the first year of his appointment. A review of the system a year later revealed that staff were over-stretched and not achieving targets set. On further investigation it was discovered that staff were running the chief executives new computer system alongside the old manual system, thereby doing double the amount of work less effectively than before!

Often natural processes in change appear on the face of it as resistance to change. Many managers make the mistake of finding ways to battle with the resistances instead of trying to understand what may underlie them and work to alleviate or minimise the effects.

Everyone reacts to change, even managers! It is important to understand how individuals' behaviour may be affected by their reactions to any change which affects them.

## Personal reactions to change

There is now a considerable body of evidence to suggest that individuals follow a common pattern of behaviour and feelings when facing and going through change. This pattern was first highlighted in the research done on reactions to bereavement, and loss and has subsequently been shown to be relevant to individuals facing any form of change or transition It is a pattern with which the majority of people can identify.

The following diagram (Figure 9.3) charts the typical reactions to change in self esteem and feelings when an individual has to face an important change.

**Figure 9.3: Personal reactions to change**

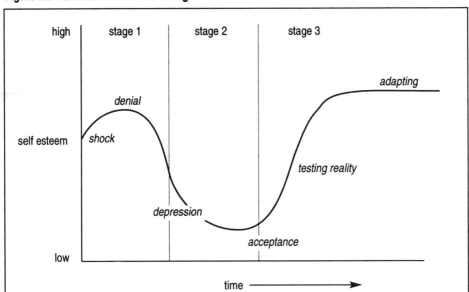

The chart shows that a person typically will go through several stages of feelings and behaviour during the process of change. It is important to note that the time taken to go through these stages will vary from person to person and be dependent on their personality, the severity of the change and, of course, other factors at play in their lives. An illustration of this is when someone discovers that their job may be made redundant. At first there is feeling of shock, which may manifest itself in a physical or psychological reaction, i.e. slowing or closing down, often the person is unable to think clearly, perform routine tasks, may even become ill. This is closely followed by a period of denial or minimisation, you may hear 'it will never happen' or 'it's a mistake' or ' they have said this before and nothing ever happened'. This period may be accompanied by a serge in activity and productivity.

The next stage is typified by a falling of self esteem, various feelings manifest themselves: anger, guilt, hopelessness, lack of control, apathy. Individuals at this stage are often unable to make decisions, or may be making them and changing them frequently. They often fantasise in a negative way about their situation, e.g. who is to blame, what the outcome will be. It is very difficult during this stage for a person to be rational and make decisions about their future, precisely when organisations may be asking them to. It is not until an individual can accept the reality of what is happening that they have reached the bottom of the curve, and can start exploring ways of dealing practically with the situation they find themselves in. It is at this stage they can look more objectively at their options and make decisions about what they will do.

The curve describes an individual's reactions to one change. In reality they may be going through a number of changes at the same time and will be experiencing numerous curves, maybe all at different stages. The depth of the curve and length of time to progress through it, will vary from person to person faced with the same change. It will be dependent on a variety of things including their personality, other circumstances, the investment they have in work etc. It is therefore difficult to predict how deeply any one individual's feelings and behaviour will be affected by a change, however there is certainty that they will be affected.

So what can a manager do to help individuals deal with change? It is obviously not practical to implement change at different rates for different people, nor would we advocate only changing when everyone is ready, however a manager can do some things to assist individuals through this roller coaster:

- Make time to listen to people, allow them to express their feelings even though you may feel they are unjustified.
- Do not expect people to make important decisions whilst they are in the initial stages of a change.
- Communicate change issues on a regular basis, remembering people's readiness to 'hear' things will vary. You will probably have to repeat the same message several times. Use several different methods, e.g. written, verbal, demonstration etc. This will help get your message across.
- Avoid surprises and keep the messages consistent and honest.
- Stick to a timetable, be clear about when consultation periods start and finish, when decisions will be made, things implemented, etc.
- Acknowledge valid objections and ideas, be prepared to adapt as you go along.
- Provide support mechanisms such as counselling or training for individuals and groups.

---

### Example 9.2: a London borough housing department

This large department decentralised into 16 neighbourhood offices. It involved virtually all staff having to cope with changes in their roles, location, reporting line etc. Some 70 posts disappeared, and subsequently those individuals had to be re-deployed. This was a major change, which demanded not only excellent planning and implementation skills but also sensitivity to the situation individuals were facing. It was recognised, some way into the change, that thought had not been given to dealing with the latter, particularly as the managers being asked to implement the changes were themselves having to face the possibility of losing their own jobs.

→

---

A number of support mechanisms were put into place to attempt to help individuals through the changes. A number of volunteers from across the department were trained to act as informal counsellors for any individuals wanting to talk through their own situations and options. This was 'off-line' and confidential. These staff counsellors were also kept up-to-date with the facts and progress of the change so they offered not only a listening ear but also factual information. A glossy news-letter was issued to all staff on a monthly basis, with information on the changes.

Specialist external career counselling was offered to the senior managers who were facing losing their jobs. A two day programme was available for those staff facing re-deployment, to help them identify the options and support them through the process. Although for many it felt chaotic and uncertain at times, the change was successfully achieved. The support that was offered to staff during the process certainly helped in that success.

Many managers would argue that there is not the time nor the resources to indulge in counselling staff. Of course, in many cases the timetable for change is beyond a manager's control. Sometimes it is important that changes are made swiftly and without the prior knowledge of the majority of staff (in cases of takeovers, or where there has been fraud or other misdemeanours). What we are saying, is that individuals in the organisation will experience the roller coaster of change whether it is before or after the change happens. As a manager you need to be aware of this and expect that there will be behavioural issues which will affect performance, and that there are things you can do either before or after the change, to help people survive the roller coaster and come out the other end positively.

### The place of training and development

Training and development has often been seen as an 'add on' activity to be considered and carried out once plans for implementation are made. This is becoming a thing of the past. Training and development activities are of key importance in not only helping individuals learn new skills but also facilitating thinking and planning change, helping change culture, and providing a useful communication channel for the organisation. Quality initiatives such as Investors in People have raised the profile of training and tied it in to business objectives. The timing and nature of training activities are crucial to their effectiveness, and therefore need to be considered early on in the change process.

Training and development activities will:

- help individuals acquire new skills;
- help individuals and teams develop new roles;
- assist culture change.

There are no hard and fast rules around training and development in the change process, each organisation will be different in terms of what they want to achieve, of the culture they are working within, and the resources they have available. Each organisation should be unique in their approach to designing and delivering effective training and development within the change process. What works for one housing organisation may well not work for another. There are, however, some useful pointers worth bearing in mind if you want to maximise the effectiveness of any training designed to assist change.

*Helping individuals acquire new skills:*

- There probably will be new or different skills being demanded of individuals and groups, in the future. *Identify* early in the process what those skills are and where there are or will be skills gaps, i.e. differences in what people can do now and what they will be required to do in the future, e.g. handling new information systems may need extra IT skills or working with different customer groups may need extra knowledge or interpersonal skills.
- The use of *focus groups* in building up a picture of the skills knowledge and attitudes that will be needed by individuals and groups in the new situation can help at this stage in making that picture as accurate as possible, with the added bonus of allowing individuals throughout the organisation to take part in shaping the future as well as becoming familiar with the aims and goals of the change.
  Focus groups are usually made up of a cross-section of staff and/or customers inside and outside the organisation who 'focus' in on a particular topic. The topic may be of a general nature such as, communication within the organisation, or be more specific, e.g. putting the detail around a new role within the organisation.
  Whichever the emphasis, the groups have a specific remit within the change process, and take responsibility for the outcomes.
- Skills *training* should not be embarked upon too early in the process. People need to see the relevance of what they are learning and be able to practice skills (see below).
- Allow *flexibility* in the detail of how things are to be done, inevitably modifications and new ideas will arise out of training sessions.
- *Get staff involved* in training design and delivery, commitment will increase and it is more likely to be relevant and effective.
- *Training takes time*, there are no short cuts. This needs to be acknowledged.

*Helping individuals and teams develop new roles:*

- People need space to make sense of new roles. Plan group activities allowing for discussion and clarification of new roles before doing more detailed skills training.

- Do not expect a training session to sort out long-running problems. Other support and actions will generally need to run alongside.

*Assisting culture change:*

- Culture change requires changes in behaviour. This needs to be demonstrated from the top. Training is not just for staff, senior managers need help to learn and develop. Culture change will be less likely where the top tier appear exempt from activities.
- Senior managers should identify their own training needs as well as those of staff and embark on development activities to help them achieve clear development goals.
- Crucial to the success of any large culture change is the appropriacy of the management style (see Chapter 10: Where am I in all this?). Senior managers should examine their prevailing style and consider what changes may be needed both in how they operate as a team and as individuals.
- Learning and changing behaviour usually takes much longer than a training session! Support is needed to help individuals reinforce what they have learned, e.g. technical support from a more 'expert' colleague through providing workplace support, support gained by regular meetings with peers to discuss problems and share tips.

## Using competencies as a framework for changing culture

When faced with major structural changes in organisations we often redefine the jobs to be done. Although much discussion often takes place about the attitudes, traits and values needed of staff to make the new organisation achieve its aims, when it comes to defining jobs, writing job descriptions and recruiting, the focus is generally on the skills and knowledge required to do the job rather than attitudes and values.

A growing number of organisations are using competencies as a base from which to work, and instead of just having a description of the tasks to be done in a post, they list the competencies needed to be successful both in the specific post and in tune with the organisation. A competency can be described as a behaviour, knowledge or skill that can be demonstrated. What is interesting about the use of competencies is that they allow the organisation to start defining the behaviours and traits which form the culture within the organisation, rather than just the tasks to be done as in traditional job descriptions. These can then become part of, not only the recruitment process but also the appraisal system and training and development of all staff. Housing organisations have a ready supply of ideas and frameworks for defining job competencies in the shape of the standards for housing NVQs and the management standards (see Chapter 10, p.184).

Competencies do not have to be yet another requirement dictated from the top of the organisation or the sole responsibility of the personnel or human resource department. Indeed following our message in the book that change is more successful if there is ownership amongst staff, some organisations have successfully used groups of staff (across the organisation) to define and develop the personal competencies expected of all staff working for the organisation. These are then included in all job definitions and added to and adapted to the requirements for specific jobs. Organisations using competencies find recruitment and selection processes far more effective, not only because of the clarity of having specific behaviours to gather evidence about but also for candidates who can more easily judge whether they measure up to a job's requirements or not. It also allows very specific development plans to be drawn up for those in post, with specific behavioural goals to measure themselves against.

## Example 9.3: Yorkshire Metropolitan Housing Association

As a result of a comprehensive organisational review, YMHA agreed a radical restructure of services and jobs. Staff were involved in the review, leading focus groups on various issues which had surfaced as a result of consultation with tenants, staff, members and stakeholders. Senior managers wanted to find a way of defining their new jobs that would embody the ethos and values they wanted to develop in the new organisation. They also needed a way of maintaining the high staff involvement. A group of employees (volunteers) worked with a consultant to identify those essential characteristics, values and behaviours that YMHA staff most valued in the people who work around them. These were the qualities that make staff effective and represent what everyone in the organisation should strive to achieve. These naturally fell into 3 areas as shown in the diagram below.

**Having commitment**
- Showing commitment to the organisation
- Working together
- Providing a quality service

**Being proactive**
- Being flexible
- Showing initiative

**Doing things right**
- Taking responsibility
- Getting the job done
- Being well organised

In each of the critical competency areas the group provided clear examples of what good and bad practice looked like, e.g. **showing commitment to the organisation**

**Negative indicators**

- Is dismissive of the aims and objectives of Yorkshire Met.

- Sometimes acts in a way which tarnishes the Yorkshire Met image.

- Works to a personal agenda and acts in a way which undermines the aims and objectives of Yorkshire Met.

- Is publicly critical of decisions taken by Yorkshire Met.

- Is rarely prepared to put him/herself out to help meet Yorkshire Met priorities.

**Positive indicators**

- Understands and supports the aims and objectives of Yorkshire Met.

- Makes choices and sets priorities to fit with Yorkshire Met aims and objectives.

- Publicly expresses support for Yorkshire Met.

- Works well within the framework of policies and procedures of Yorkshire Met.

- Is concerned about the image of Yorkshire Met.

- Acts professionally.

- Will often put Yorkshire Met needs before personal preferences.

- Stands by unpopular decisions which are good for Yorkshire Met in the longer term.

The results were published in the form of a development guide for employees and given to each member of staff. Recruitment to new posts in the organisation was based on competencies including personal competencies. They will also form the base of appraisal and development plans. So far, competencies have received a very positive response, both managers and staff pleased to have something so practical to base their practice on. The key to the success is that it is about, specifically for, and relevant to, YMHA and its aims.

## Communication during change

Organisations do not change, people do. The less individuals know about changes, the more they will assume, the more suspicious they will become and inevitably the more resistant.

It is clear that to make any change effective, there will have to be a degree of communication with staff. Many academics and consultants will argue that the greater the involvement of staff in the change the greater the commitment to the organisation and the better the performance (e.g. Peters and Waterman, 1982). However, when considering communication and involvement strategies during change it is wise to look at where the organisation is at present.

**Figure 9.3: Escalator of participation in change**

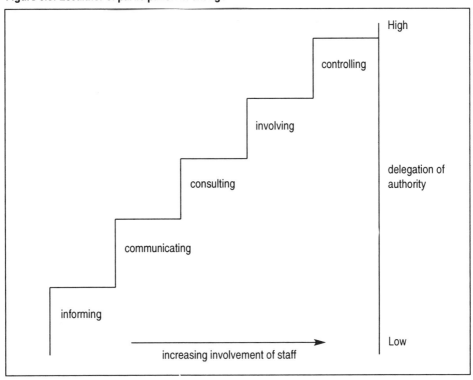

The labels used in this diagram (Figure 9.3) were used in a study by the Manchester Business School on behalf of the Department of Employment (1992) which analysed the various methods of involving staff which are used by organisations.

**Informing:** newsletters notice boards, team briefing, downward communication systems. Decisions made at the top and communicated downwards.

**Communicating:** team briefing with feedback mechanisms, staff surveys, suggestion schemes, methods which help management know what staff feel and think, systems which enable information to flow downwards and upwards.

**Consulting:** asking for opinions about issues, management taking them into consideration in their decision-making process, information flowing about the decisions and how they are made.

**Involving:** giving individuals, groups and teams limited authority for decisions.

**Controlling:** collective working, joint ownership, co-operatives.

Figure 9.3 illustrates different levels of involvement and their relationship to delegation of authority. It is drawn as an escalator, suggesting that the progress needs to be incremental in order to increase staff involvement effectively. It is difficult to suddenly jump from being an organisation which has always informed its people in a top down fashion, to one which delegates decision-making and responsibility to groups and teams. Individuals in the organisation will be suspicious of such a change and also, lack the knowledge and skills to operate in such a way. A change of culture in this fashion will require time to help people learn new skills and develop trust in the new way of working. Equally, the organisation with a culture of consultation and high degree of delegated authority will find it extremely difficult to go back down the escalator and introduce a change in a top down fashion. In general, people in organisations like involvement. Whatever the stage on the escalator, it is harder for people to give up the level of involvement they are used to, than to increase it or work within the prevailing culture.

Consultation comes in many guises in organisations. At one end of the spectrum is the housing department who have been 'consulting' on a re-organisation for three years and at the other end the housing association chief executive whose idea of consultation was to circulate to staff the final version of the new structure for comment before the relevant committee meeting a week later. The reasons for these differing strategies and styles are numerous, factors such as history, culture, personalities, and external pressures all play a part. No one style will be right for every organisation, however the costs of getting it wrong are great.

**Key considerations for communicating during change:**

- Before you embark on a process, be clear where your organisation is on the escalator.
- You will need to increase the level of communication in the organisation during change.
- Be clear yourself and be clear with the organisation, about what methods and levels of involvement you are using; explain the terminology you are using and what that means in a practical sense.
- Increase the level of involvement incrementally, don't try to jump ahead too quickly. People need to be supported and trained in active involvement.
- Once on the escalator it is difficult to go back down. Once staff are used to participating in decision-making, reversing the process can lead to problems.
- Managers need to be able to give up power and authority. Managers may well believe in the principle of delegated authority but when it comes to the crunch find it difficult to 'let go'.
- The organisation needs to address how it deals with mistakes. Staff will not wish to take on responsibilities and authority if mistakes are seen to be punished.

# Summary

After reading this chapter you should now:

- Be able to use force field analysis to plot and assess critically all the factors helping and hindering a specific change, and be able to plan an agenda of actions needed to progress it.
- Understand how individuals react to change and how a manager or leader of change can assist by: using good communication skills and strategies; by phasing change and keeping to time scales and deadlines; and offering counselling and support.
- Understand the importance of people in the organisation owning changes that need to take place and be able to gain their commitment to the change by communicating well and involving them in development and implementation.
- Understand that every organisation is different and will require different responses and actions to enable effective change. You should now have a range of tools, techniques and strategies that can be drawn upon, as appropriate, to progress specific organisational changes in the most effective way.

# Further reading

Adam, J. (1976) *Transition: Understanding and Managing Personal Change*, Martin Robertson.

Andersen, E., Grode, K., Hardy, T., Turner, J. (1987) *Goal Directed Project Management*, Kogan Page.

Harvey Jones, J. (1988) *Making it Happen: Reflections on Leadership*, Collins.

Haynes, M. (1990) *Project Management*, Kogan Page.

Leigh, A. (1988) *Effective Change*, Institute of Personnel Management.

LGMB. (1995) *NVQs and National Standards, Planning for Success*, LGMB.

Management Standards (1997) *Level 5 Operational Management*; (1997) *Level 5, Strategic Management*, Management Charter Institute.

Marchington, Goodman, Wilkinson and Ackers, Manchester School of Business Management (1992) *New Developments in Employee Involvement*, Department of Employment.

McCalman, J. and Paton, R. (1992) *Change Management*, PCP.

Moss Kanter, R. (1992) *The Change Masters*, Routledge.

Peters, T.J. and Waterman, R.H. (1982) *In Search of Excellence*, Harper Row.

Plant, R. (1987) *Managing Change*, Gower.

# CHAPTER 10:
# Where am I in all this?

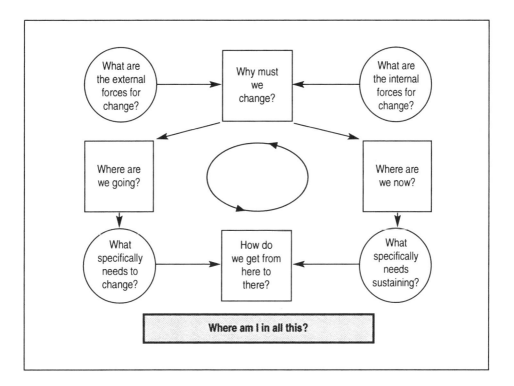

Objectives:
This chapter will enable you to:

- have an understanding of your role, its demands and how they might change;
- be clearer about your strengths and weaknesses and be able to identify how you want to develop in the future;
- understand the importance of finding a mentor/listening ear, to talk through issues and concerns;
- be clear about your values and principles;
- understand the importance of making time for yourself – ensuring space for reflection, personal development, rest and respite.

# Introduction

We put a great deal of effort into analysing, planning and implementing changes in organisations. Unfortunately, the last things that managers consider when leading change are the changes they face themselves. These could include new tasks and responsibilities, acquiring new skills, new colleagues and working relationships, increased workload (or conversely decreased workload!).

We often don't find time to ask questions of ourselves until it is too late.

- What effects are the processes having on our motivation and energy?
- Do we have the skills, knowledge and personal competencies to operate in the new situation?
- Are we able to cope with the demands made on our time and energy?
- How do we need to change to meet the new demands?
- Do I want to be here?

The one thing we can be certain of is that there will be change, and change will affect everyone. We have already looked at the impact change has on self esteem. The manager is not immune to these reactions and will inevitably go through the roller coaster of emotions during the change process, often in advance of others in the organisation. The roller coaster will be more acute where the manager is facing uncertainty about their own job, for example, in large-scale re-organisations or changes such as CCT where survival of the organisation is a very real issue! These feelings will inevitably affect our behaviour as managers. They can manifest themselves in many ways, the trick is to be able to recognise when our own behaviour is becoming dysfunctional to the organisation, the people around us and ourselves. The 'fight or flight' response to stress or threat is one of the more recognisable reactions. The manager with the fight response, sees every situation as a battlefield and goes to war regardless of the potential outcomes and casualties. This manager soon loses all sense of which battles are worth fighting and expends much energy on lost causes.

We have all witnessed or experienced the flight response, where the reaction to a difficult situation is for managers to bury themselves in their work, procrastinate, avoid making decisions, pass work up or down the line, or more obviously, go on leave at the crucial time. We all have these responses to change so what can we do to balance the needs and demands of effectively managing organisational change whilst coping with the personal demands those changes are making on you?

This chapter will examine your role as a manager and leader in the process of change. It will focus on you as an individual as well as a manager of change, what you need to consider in order to develop and sustain yourself and some practical ideas for surviving.

# Your role as a manager

Whether you are new to management or are an experienced manager, one of the primary keys to working effectively is to understand what your role actually is. You will of course have a job description which will outline tasks and responsibilities, but it is unlikely that it will tell you whether your role is strategic or operational. This is an extremely important distinction which will affect the way in which you tackle activities, your involvement with others in the organisation and how you approach and manage change.

**Figure 10.1: Basic roles**

| Operational Management | Strategic Management |
|---|---|
| determining objectives | forward planning |
| planning and organising | visioning the future |
| communicating with subordinates | leading initiatives |
| communicating with senior manager | adapting the organisation to change |
| controlling staff | identifying and analysing opportunities |
| motivating | and threats, determining responses |
| controlling costs | ensuring that the organisation stays 'healthy' |
| maximising productivity | |

This is not an exhaustive list but hopefully it is sufficient to show the types of activity associated with strategic and operational management. In reality, few managers in an organisation will be totally strategic, possibly only the most senior manager. The majority of senior managers will have a mixture of strategic and operational responsibilities, with the majority of middle and first line managers being operational.

The difficulty for most managers is making the transition from being operational to being strategic.

---

## Exercise 10.1: Are you a strategic or an operational manager?

Complete the short questionnaire by ticking the statements that best describe your behaviour at work.

1.  I like to do jobs myself. Delegation takes time.

2.  We would not get through the work if I did not help with getting the task done.

3.  I usually set objectives for my team.

→

---

4. It is important that I review the achievement of our objectives.

5. I don't like to be too remote from the front line.

6. When a new idea is put forward I always consider whether it will work on the ground.

7. I can do most of the jobs my team can.

8. I tend to challenge the way we do things.

9. I do not have a clear sense of where the organisation is going.

10. I encourage having explicit values.

11. I am actively involved in developing my organisation.

12. I seek to achieve clarity in policy-making.

13. I make time to review the organisation's strengths and weaknesses.

14. I regularly consider the impact of current trends on our business.

15. When new ideas are raised I consider how they fit with strategic plans before thinking about whether they will work.

16. I always let my staff report directly to others on matters for which they are responsible.

17. Sometimes current performance has to be sacrificed for longer term gains.

18. I am confident my staff can deal with most operational problems that occur.

19. I never rule out the possibility of radical change.

20. I do not like to have detailed information on how things are done.

The first ten statements are typical behaviours of a manager concerned with the getting the task done, the remaining statements describe those of a manager concerned with strategic issues. In reality of course, the majority of managers have a mixture of operational and strategic roles. First line managers will only have a small proportion of their time devoted to strategic issues, usually confined to specific times when the organisation is reviewing itself. As managers become more senior, more time should be spent on strategic activities, and those holding the most senior posts should be continually concerned with strategic issues. If the balance of your particular responses seem inappropriate for your role, you may need to examine further why this is so.

- Is it your preferred style of working? (see section on leadership style)
- Is it a result of the particular circumstances in your organisation?
- Is it a pressure of work issue?

Understanding and having the tools to operate strategically are important, but most senior managers who come on our programmes say they do not find the time to think, plan and manage strategically. The pressures of senior management are great and often 'being strategic' gets lost in the day-to-day pressures of managing the business. Being able to stop being operational is critical to becoming a strategic manager.

### Understanding the demands of your role

There are several methods of analysing the demands your role makes on your time. Traditional approaches involve making time logs, doing detailed analysis of how you are spending your time and deciding where efficiencies can be made. This is a very valid approach but it is time consuming and tends to deal with your role as it is or has been. It allows you to examine the detail of your job and the way you operate, yet often fails to give an overview of your role which is necessary during change. A quicker and more general approach is one which we call *Role Amoeba*. A role amoeba is a pictorial representation of your role and future role. It can be done in a very rough and ready way or can be done more scientifically using actual time log data.

The amoeba is made up of a series of lines radiating from a central point. Each line represents an area of work, there should be between 6 and 12 areas of work, their precise nature obviously unique to, and defined by, the individual manager.

Using a 'guesstimate', or more detailed data, a point should be marked on each line which represents the proportion of time spent on that particular area of work. The points can then be joined up revealing a shape which represents your role in terms of total time spent.

This shape is like an amoeba, which as it moves changes its shape as one 'limb' extends another part of it retracts; its volume must always remain the same (Figure 10.2). If changes are required in the time spent on specific areas of work the area or volume of the amoeba should remain the same, assuming that the total time devoted to work needs to remain the same.

**Figure 10.2: Role amoeba of a housing manager in a medium-sized housing association**

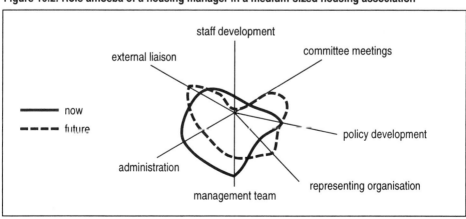

In the example above the housing manager, has to spend more time on external liaison in the next few months as the association is working in partnership on a community initiative. That time will have to be found from somewhere. Normally managers' squeeze and mould their time as they go along, more often than not leading to tasks and relationships suffering in the process. Drawing the role amoeba allows the housing manager to consider where that time will come from. The total area of the amoeba needs to remain the same if this manager does not want to extend working hours. The decision in this instance was to spend less time on administration. The tasks in the administrative line, of course, will not just disappear and will need to be reallocated or maybe re-appraised.

A role amoeba is a very simple tool to assist you examine your role. Where your role will substantially change in the future, a second amoeba can be superimposed over the present one.

---

**Exercise 10.2: Having drawn an amoeba, questions to be asked are:**

- What happens to the work in the workload that is being reduced?

- Is it possible/desirable to increase or decrease the total area of the amoeba?

- What effect do changes made to your amoeba have on others in the organisation?

- Do you need to do what you are doing?

---

This graphic representation of a manager's role can be extremely useful in a number of ways:

1) It can be used individually to think through the effect of changes to role.
2) It can be used with a team to show how shifting tasks and responsibilities will affect members of the team.
3) For those who like accuracy and detail it can be used with a time logging system to graphically illustrate use of time.

### *Workload implications of changing your role*

Instant change only happens on paper, and there is a lot of that during organisational change. The diagram below (Figure 10.3) illustrates the impact on workload when changing a job or role within an organisation.

---

**Figure 10.3: Workload variation during change**

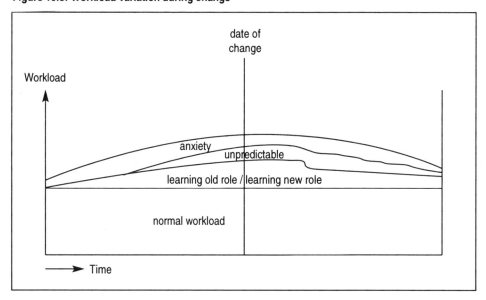

The decision to reorganise or change may well have defined specific dates on which the change will take place but the process of change begins before the formal date and will end a long time after. Change has to be both learned and emotionally adjusted to; neither aspect of which happens instantly. It is managing the realities of this gradual process of transition that requires a distinctive competence of management, one that is complementary to that of 'running' with the organisation.

What is being demanded of you during change is not more of the same, i.e. not just an increase in workload. There are three aspects to the change. First, in any aspect of change there is **additional workload**. Work needs reallocating and learning by others. More often than not individuals and groups need support taking on new functions. However good training, instruction and procedural manuals are, inevitably there will be areas of the job that are 'in the heads' of the previous post-holder. Officially the tasks have gone but they live on and take up time, in the form of providing support and information to those taking over the tasks. Indeed some individuals have difficulty in 'letting go' of their old tasks and responsibilities, thus they will carry an even greater burden for a long time.

You need to learn and adjust to the 'new' needs of the job. The greater the difference between old and new, the greater the literal overload during the transition period. Individuals get more concerned with getting the job done rather than how it gets done, or with the people concerned. Often this creates its own tensions and blockages.

**Anxiety** is the second factor at play, it is the anxiety that change itself engenders. Change produces anxiety in most of us: fear of unknown tasks and relationships, fear of being unhappy, fear of failure, and many others. The anxiety generated makes us all feel more cautious and even defensive. Sometimes it literally prevents us from thinking or getting on practically with a task. Potential work problems get deferred until they emerge forcefully, or indeed emerge on other people's agendas. The task for managers is to recognise the power of anxiety and help moderate its effect both individually and collectively. This sensitivity is required just when managers are concerned with 'getting the job done'.

The third aspect is dealing with the **unpredictable**. However much planning and preparation is done, unpredictable events, problems and hitches will inevitably arise. These have to be dealt with and create an extra burden on the new role.

In addition to the 'operational' and 'structural' issues which need resolving there are some less obvious factors related to workload which need consideration in preparation and implementation of change.

**Suggestions for minimising potential disruptions to effective working during change**
Generally in planning:

- Allow time for 'old' post-holders to support new ones during the bedding-in period.
- Allow for a dip in normal performance during hand-over period, but prioritise key performance targets.
- Ensure individuals and teams have time before and after to establish and agree roles, tasks and relationships.

Personally:

- Anxiety will diminish the ability to perform to full capability so do not expect to 'fire on all cylinders' from day one.
- Form a link with the person previously doing the job.
- Put effort into establishing working relationships with new colleagues.
- Clarify and agree with colleagues, soon after the change, expectations of each others' new roles and how you will formally relate to one another (e.g. information needed, responsibilities etc.).

### *Clarifying your role*

One useful mechanism for facilitating discussions about role is using the '**loose/ tight**' concept. This captures a crucial idea in management which has often been blurred in the past. It is a way of describing the balance that there needs to be between what is defined for a manager by the organisation (tight properties) and what is left to the manager's discretion (loose properties) as to how they fulfil the relevant functions (see Figure 10.4). There is, more often than not, also a middle ground in which there will always be negotiation between managers about what happens in particular situations. As a manager facing change, using this concept as a basis for discussion can be most helpful in clarifying what is required, where you can exercise discretion and determine what needs further definition or clarification. See Example 10.1.

**Figure 10.4: Loose and tight aspects of a management role**

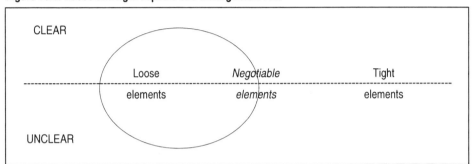

**Example 10.1: Case study: Regional Director, Housing Corporation and Performance Review Manager**

A re-organisation in 1993 decentralised the Performance Audit function at the Housing Corporation resulting in the regional Performance Review Managers (PRM) reporting directly to Regional Directors (RD).

To all intents and purposes tasks to be done remained the same. A policy and advice service remained at headquarters and in the regions the performance audit was intended to remain at 'arms length' from the other functions of the regional office. The danger was that PRMs would continue as semi-autonomous and separate from the rest of the regional office, especially as most Regional Directors had little knowledge of Performance Review principles and practice.

Recognising the potential for conflict both between the sections within the regional office and the PRM and RD, the regional Performance Review Manager in one region sought an early meeting with the his Regional Director to clarify roles, areas of responsibility and how they were to work together. This meeting allowed both parties to talk not only about some of the more sensitive issues such as decision-making responsibilities and roles, but also about some of the more practical working methods such as what information they required from each other, how frequently and on what basis they should have meetings, what performance measures they should agree. The agreed way of working was documented and reviewed after a period of time. The transition went smoothly.

→

> The Regional Director said, "It was the first time I have ever done this in a structured way, usually you end up having this discussion some way into a change, often as a result of things going wrong. It is so easy to launch into the detail of tasks to be done, problems, issues and crises. In the past I had viewed it as somehow taking time for thrashing out what seems obvious. However, unless you do have these discussions then both parties end up working on assumptions which in the long term become problematic. I learned a lot from this and have now made it a practice to have this sort of discussion with all staff directly reporting to me and with those to whom I report."

## Knowing your strengths and weaknesses

The culture of the organisation was discussed in Chapter 5. The importance of establishing what the present culture of the organisation is and agreeing what it should be and needs to be in the future, cannot be underestimated.

Changing the culture is complex and often a very long process. One key factor in that process is the style of leadership within the organisation and as a manager or leader in that organisation you need to know what your style is, and whether you need to develop it in a particular direction. Many efforts to change organisational culture have run aground due to the lack of awareness of the senior managers about their personal style and its effects on the organisation, see Example 10.2.

### Example 10.2: A London borough housing department

The department was attempting to reorganise into a more locally accountable, multi-disciplinary area based structure. The old regime was recognised as bureaucratic and hierarchical, with decisions being pushed as far up the structure as possible. In a meeting to explain the new structure and culture, the Director of Housing talked enthusiastically about increased responsibility for decision-making at area level, the ability to get on with the job without constantly seeking approval and taking risks in doing things differently if it was thought it could work. The culture needed was a learning one in which individuals should take responsibility, successes acknowledged and mistakes learned from, not punished.

This of course, caused some lively debate and a few fears felt by members of staff were brought out into the open. The Director encouraged this openness as a demonstration of the new culture being developed. The following day the Assistant Director of Housing rang several of the individuals who had raised issues and told them their behaviour was unacceptable and that in future they should not speak out at such meetings. Of course, the staff saw this as evidence that nothing would change and the old regime would live on despite the rhetoric. The Assistant Director was completely in favour of the change but totally unaware that his style was not in tune with the new culture.

Any time you seek to influence the behaviour of another person you are engaging in an act of leadership. Leadership style is a pattern of behaviours you use when trying to influence the behaviour of others, as *perceived by them*. While your perceptions of your own behaviour and its impact on others is interesting and important, it tells you only how you *intend* to act. Unless it matches the perceptions of those you are trying to influence it is not very helpful (as can be seen in the example above where the intention and actions were perceived differently by manager and staff). If you see yourself as a people-orientated manager, but your staff think you are hard nosed, task-orientated person, whose perception of reality will they act on – yours or theirs? Obviously their own!

There are many theories about leadership style and methods of assessing your own style. One of the most useful, 'Situational Leadership', was developed by Ken Blanchard some 20 years ago (Hersey and Blanchard, 1992). As a result of further research it has recently been reviewed and updated and is now called 'Situational Leadership 2' (confirming that the original basis of the theory is still valid). The theory supports the idea that leadership is not an either/or continuum, i.e. autocratic or democratic, theory x or theory y (McGregor, 1960). It suggests that effective leaders are able to be flexible in their style according to the needs of the individuals or groups and the needs of the task in hand. Blanchard's research showed that leadership styles tend to be a combination of directive and supportive behaviour.

*Directive behaviour* being defined as the extent to which a leader tells followers what to do, where, when and how to do it. It is behaviour which structures, controls and supervises. *Supportive behaviour* is the extent to which a leader listens, provides support and encouragement, facilitates interaction and involves followers in decision-making. It is behaviour which praises, listens and facilitates.

Blanchard identifies four typical leadership styles as illustrated in the diagram below.

**Figure 10.5: Situational leadership**

The four leadership styles

| | | |
|---|---|---|
| high | | |
| Supportive behaviour | high supportive<br>low directive<br><br>**S3** | high supportive<br>high directive<br><br>**S2** |
| | **S4**<br>low directive<br>low supportive | **S1**<br>high directive<br>low supportive |
| low | Directive behaviour | high |

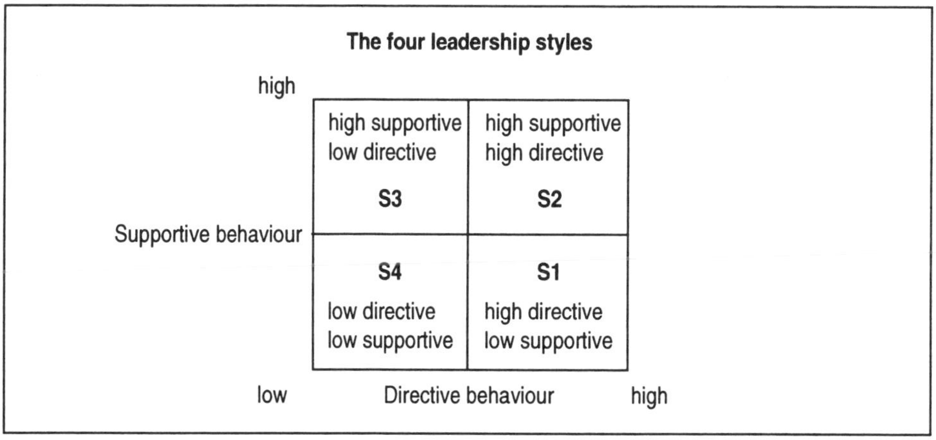

**Directing S1:** this style is characterised by high directive behaviour and low supportive behaviour. Leaders define the roles of followers, tell them what tasks to do, when, where and how to do them. Solutions and decisions are announced, communication is largely one way, and implementation is closely supervised. This style is effective when the followers are lacking in competence or new to a task, but have high commitment to the task or organisation. An example of this being an appropriate style to use is when a new piece of legislation needs to be implemented, e.g. in a benefits section when there is a change in Housing Benefit regulations.

**Coaching S2:** this style is characterised by high supportive behaviour and high directive behaviour. The leader provides a great deal of direction with ideas but also attempts to hear the followers' feelings about decisions as well as their ideas and suggestions. Control over decision-making remains with the leader. This style is appropriate for groups or individuals who have some familiarity with the task but either lack motivation, sufficient knowledge or confidence to take responsibility for initiating ideas or making day-to-day decisions. Examples of this style can often be found in managers leading less experienced housing officer teams.

**Supporting S3:** this style is characterised by high supportive behaviour and low directive behaviour. The focus for day-to-day decision-making and problem-solving is with the followers. This style is appropriate for groups and individuals who have a thorough knowledge of the task and ability to work without supervision, but whose confidence needs boosting or reassuring. Often those working closely with clients and who do much of their work 'away' from base, such as advisory and tenant liaison workers, require this type of leadership.

**Delegating S4:** Characterised by low supportive behaviour and low directive behaviour. The leader discusses problems with subordinates until agreement is reached on problem definition: the decision-making process is in the hands of the followers. Followers are allowed to 'run their own show'. This style of leadership is appropriate for any group or individual who has a thorough knowledge of their work area and the skill to operate on their own initiative. They do need to be motivated and confident about working in this way, and it needs to be an accepted way of operating within the organisation. Most typically this type of leadership is seen when groups of 'professionals' are being managed, however, there is no reason why it cannot be applicable to any 'mature' group of staff.

So the four styles are valid in a variety of situations. The key skill of leadership is to be able to adapt your style as appropriate. Everyone has preferred ways of working and individuals have preferred ways of being managed. This can work well where there is a match, and in stable situations. However, the challenge in the housing arena today is being able to deal with change. Leaders and staff are having to cope with a multitude of changes, both desirable and less desirable.

An appropriate flexible style is not only desirable but essential. As a leader you need to be able to develop your staff maybe from a position of low competence or low commitment to one of high commitment and competence. You can only do this by adapting your style to assist their development and growth.

### Learning from experience

Up until recently, senior managers in housing had little guidance about what they actually should be doing on a day-to-day basis, how they should operate and the skills they should display. Of course, the Chartered Institute of Housing offered sound professional guidance on specific issues, but little has existed for say a new chief executive or director of housing to use as a guide for developing their competence in leadership and strategic matters. Senior managers often say that although you can learn a lot from managing departments or functions, surviving and succeeding at the top is different and has to be learnt 'on-the-job'.

A manager's success in leading an organisation is closely linked with their ability to learn from current experiences. People learn in different ways, and it is important to recognise, as a manager, the way you tend to learn and how that might speed or inhibit your own development.

Honey and Mumford's detailed research on how people learn, identified four styles of learning (Honey and Mumford, 1986). The next diagram shows the four styles as points on two axis (Figure 10.5).

**Figure 10.5: Learning styles**

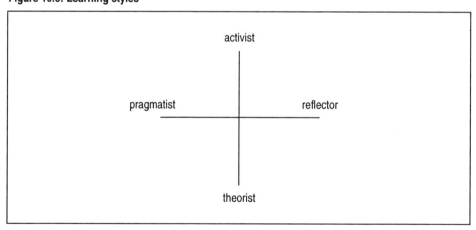

The *activists* involve themselves fully in new experiences. They enjoy the 'here and now', are open minded, and not sceptical which tends to make them enthusiastic about anything new. They often tackle problems by brainstorming, and tend to be bored with implementation and long term consolidation. Drawing out learning points and reflecting on what needs to be done as a result are not strong points of activists.

*Reflectors* collect and analyse data about their experiences in order to reach a definitive conclusion about a situation. They will take a back seat in meetings and enjoy observing other people in action. When they act it is a result of considering every angle and seeing things in the 'wide picture'. They do not enjoy fast action or having to make quick decisions.

*Theorists* tend to be detached, analytical and dedicated to rational objectivity. They prefer to maximise certainty and feel uncomfortable with subjective judgement, lateral thinking and anything flippant. They like to form models and theories about the way things should work.

*Pragmatists* are keen on trying out ideas and techniques to see if they work in practice. They don't like beating about the bush and get impatient with ruminating and open-ended discussions. Their maxim is, 'if it works it's good'.

We all have a little of each of these styles but evidence shows that we tend to prefer one or two of the styles and feel uncomfortable or less natural with the others. It is important that as a manager you know your preferred learning style in order to match your style to the right situations and experiences. A senior manager in an organisation will not have the luxury of choosing appropriate activities to match their style. It is also important to develop the styles you are less comfortable with to maximise learning and development opportunities within the context of day-to-day work.

---

**Exercise 10.3**

Consider your personal learning style.

Where would you put yourself on the diagram above?

Where would you put members of your team?

What implications might this have for the way you operate and learn as an individual and a group?

---

## *Using management standards to assess your performance*

Self knowledge such as understanding the learning and leadership styles you exhibit is a key factor in developing yourself as a leader. What many managers have sought over the years is a definitive guide or checklist of what they should actually be doing. The Management Charter Initiative, is the national standard setting body for management across all sectors. It has defined and set management standards at four levels, supervisory, first-line, middle and senior management. The Management Charter Initiative defines senior managers as members of the board or governing body of the organisation, and those who report to it. The Senior Management Standards set out the skills, behaviours and knowledge which a senior manager requires to perform effectively.

They are structured into three parts as shown in the diagram below:

**Figure 10.7: Structures for management standards**

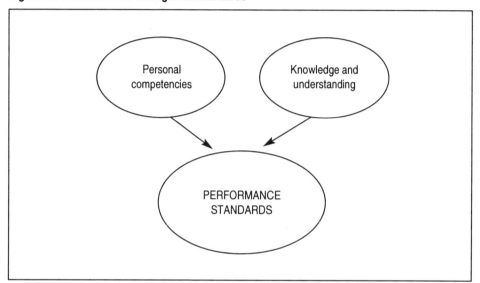

The national standards describe the repertoire of skills which senior managers may use to achieve good performance. These are called *personal competencies*, they include skills such as judgement, communication, strategic perspective. A complete list can be found later in Exercise 10.4.

The *knowledge and understanding* outlined is that which is required to sustain good performance. It covers technical knowledge such as specific legislation, finance and accounting etc., knowledge needed to understand specific situations such as relevant local and environmental factors, concepts and theory, and finally understanding relationships.

Both these elements underpin the *performance standards* which specify the management activities and processes and the outcomes which constitute good performance. The Senior Management Standards define the key purpose of senior management as being *to develop and implement strategies to further the organisation's mission.*

The performance standards are grouped into four key areas (see Figure 10.8).

**Figure 10.8: Performance Standard groupings**

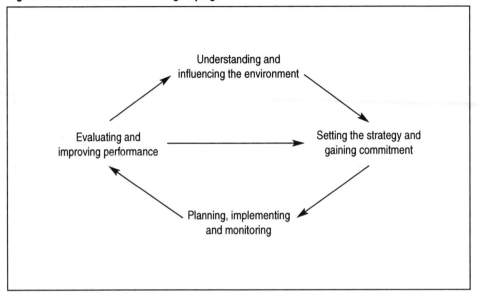

Within each of these areas performance criteria are specified which describe in detail the processes and outcomes that a senior manager is expected to achieve for good performance. They are set in a general context and have to be interpreted within a housing and specific organisational setting.

The Management Standards at all levels, i.e. supervisory, line, middle and senior, are gradually being integrated into professional bodies' qualifications. You can, however, work with them in a number of ways:

1.  Individually to credit your current competence by building up a portfolio showing how you work to the relevant standards.
2.  In a management team to assist in improving performance by setting agreed standards for the team.
3.  As a base for appraisal of managers.
4.  As a guide for setting criteria for recruitment of managerial staff.
5.  As a starting point for some self assessment and self development.

**Exercise**

Below is a list of the personal competencies identified by the Management Charter Initiative as being critical to the success of a strategic manager. Each competence is supported by a list of behaviours which demonstrate that specific competence. Read through them carefully and then rate yourself on a scale 1-5 as to whether you think you display those behaviours in normal circumstances: 1 never; 2 rarely; 3 sometimes; 4 often; 5 always. Repeat the exercise, this time in the context of how you tend to behave in a crisis.

What do you need to improve on? What do you tend to lose when in crisis mode? This is a self assessment, to get a more comprehensive view of your competencies ask a colleague, your manager or a member of your staff to fill it in about you. You may see different results. Examine the differences. Maybe what you are doing is not being received in the way that you are intending. Similarities in scores may reinforce your views of your strengths and weaknesses.

---

## Exercise 10.4

**Personal competencies**                                          **Rating 1-5**

*Strategic Vision*
- Works towards a vision of the future based on a strategic perspective.      ..........
- Acts with good understanding of how different parts, needs or functions of the organisation and its environment fit together.      ..........
- Clearly relates goals and actions to the strategic aims of the business.      ..........
- Takes opportunities when they arise to achieve longer term needs.      ..........

*Achievement Focus*
- Sets high quality goals that are demanding of self and others.      ..........
- Sets objectives and priorities in uncertain and complex situations.      ..........
- Tackles risks and takes decisive action.      ..........
- Focuses personal attention on specific details that are critical to the success of a key event.      ..........

*Communication*
- Conveys difficult ideas and problems in a way that aids understanding.      ..........
- Recognises and responds to the needs and feelings of others.      ..........

*Information Search*
- Pushes for concrete information in an ambiguous situation.      ..........
- Seeks information from multiple sources to clarify a situation.      ..........
- Checks the validity of own thinking with others.      ..........

*Influencing others*
- Uses a variety of means to influence others.      ..........
- Creates and prepares strategies for influencing others.      ..........
- Understands the culture of the organisation and acts to work within it or influence it.      ..........
- Develops and uses networks to trade information, support or build other resources.      ..........

*Building teams*
- Keeps others informed about plans and progress.      ..........
- Builds a desire to work together and builds co-operation within a team.      ..........
- Builds ownership of controversial decisions by involving others in the decision-making process.      ..........
- Evaluates people's capability to do the job and takes action.      ..........

→

---

---

*Self confidence*
- Acts in an assured and unhesitating manner when faced with a challenge. ...........
- Takes the leading role in initiating action and making decisions. ...........
- Maintains beliefs, commitment and effort in spite of setbacks or opposition. ...........

*Judgment*
- Identifies the most important issues in a complex situation. ...........
- Identifies implications, consequences or casual relationships in a situation. ...........
- Uses a range of ideas to explain the actions, needs and motives of others. ...........
- Focuses on facts, problems and solutions when handling an emotional situation. ...........
- Uses instinct and intuition to assess situations and people. ...........
- Identifies new patterns and interprets events in new ways. ...........

---

## The listening ear

In the current climate of change we are facing issues and situations of which we have no previous experience. The complexity of work is increasing, relationships with peers, colleagues and contacts are changing in nature. The juxtaposition of 'competition' and 'collaboration' within housing has affected traditional relationships both externally and internally.

"It's lonely at the top", is a maxim we have heard used by many senior managers in housing and it appears to becoming increasingly true. Even the most self perceptive of us get it wrong, we get stuck in our ways of behaving, we only see things from a particular perspective. No wonder we find it difficult to be creative or find a different way forward or a solution to a problem.

Developing a mentoring relationship or relationships with another individual or group can provide that other perspective we so often lack in our day-to-day operational work.

Our experience running senior management programmes has shown that one of the aspects most valued by managers is the opportunity to discuss, reflect, bounce ideas off and seek advice from their peers. Although we often assume these opportunities exist at meetings, conferences and in the normal daily contact with others, this appears not to be the case. Mentors or support groups can be formed informally as a result of common interests or activities such as attendance on courses, participation in particular projects, or sharing specialist interest areas. Participation can also be on a more formal basis such as belonging to an action learning group, having a formal mentoring system within the organisation or undertaking a course in which having a mentor is a requirement.

Such supportive relationships whether formal or informal usually need a degree of thought and structure, to make them useful and productive.

Aspects to consider when thinking about establishing a mentoring relationship include:

- Agreement about confidentiality (particularly if there is a work relationship).
- The boundaries of the subject matter (just work or including personal issues).
- Is the relationship mentor/mentee or co-mentoring?
- The aim of the relationship, e.g. to improve performance, for career development, counselling, listening ear, sharing knowledge.
- The respective learning styles of those involved (the impact and usefulness of contrasting or similar styles).
- Time boundaries, including frequency of meetings.
- How to review the success of the relationship.

### Putting it in perspective

It is very easy to become seduced by housing, the politics of it, the practicality of it, the issues and the difficulties. Not only do we become absorbed by these, we also get embroiled with the organisation in terms of its performance, structures, interpersonal relationships etc. Many of those in housing, work long hours, and often spend non-work time on housing related voluntary activities. Many housing people are no longer energised by the challenges, they are feeling stressed. The danger of 'burnout' is ever present, and the symptoms of high stress levels are beginning to be seen in housing organisations. As a manager what can you do to maintain your energy and enthusiasm and prevent yourself from becoming subsumed by it all?

### Career rainbow

When working with individuals and groups on career development issues, the common perception of career is linear. That is people perceive themselves as being on a progressive career ladder, those involved in housing see it as a housing ladder. You enter the profession at the lower levels and progress upwards, through front-line to management then on to senior levels, often in the same or similar organisations. In reality this is how many have 'made it' to senior management. You are defined by the job you do and the type of organisation you work for. We are however in turbulent times, jobs at every level are no longer 'safe bets', the skills and knowledge needed to operate in ever changing settings are different from those needed in the past. It seems for the first time, very senior managers are losing their jobs for political, performance and financial reasons.

Many organisations are seeing it as advantageous to pay fees for work to be done rather than employing individuals. Consultancy and short term contracts are now common place in housing. Part time, job share, reduced hours are no longer terms just reserved for lower level posts.

Many senior managers have been made redundant and it is clear that there is no shortage of short term contracts, and individuals can hold several such contracts at a time. Financially, in the short term they are better off, but the long term security is missing. For some, this way of working has a lot of benefits, not the least of which is the lessening of the stress factor associated with full time permanent senior management.

Public, voluntary, private, terms previously so clear in housing, are becoming blurred. Some individuals, previously defining themselves as public sector workers are finding themselves in the private sector as a result of CCT or LSVT. They are no longer so clear about their work identity and image. These changes can bring into question values people have held for most of their working lives.

It is becoming unhelpful to perceive 'career' in terms of a ladder to climb up or slide down, as clearly more and more in housing have non-traditional models of working. Charles Handy (1989) talks of 'portfolio lives'. He refers not just to holding a number of different contracts for paid employment but also to the fact that we should consider 'career' in terms of life career.

Another writer, Donald Super (1981), puts forward the concept of a 'career rainbow'. The colours of the rainbow represent different roles you have in life: worker, child, parent, citizen, spouse, learner, etc. Super suggests that career should be viewed as a totality and that as in a rainbow, different colours at different times will be more or less prominent. So it is important to consider the significance of your other roles in life at any particular time, for example, the demands of a growing family often come at precisely the time when the demands of the job are at their height.

Keeping a balance is important for most individuals and those around them. A holistic view of career helps individuals to allow themselves to make decisions, which in traditional 'career ladder' terms may not make sense, but in terms of fulfilment and peace of mind are the most logical. Those decisions may be relatively small, such as being clear about the limits of your working day or carving out time each week to do a sport or hobby. They may be big decisions such as resigning from a secure job, undertaking a course of study, changing career direction, taking a sabbatical. The patterns of our working lives are fundamentally changing and as individuals and managers, we need to amend our view of career not only in order to make sense of the world around us but also to take some control over our own futures.

# Summary

After reading this chapter you should now:

- Know whether you tend to operate as a strategic or operational manager and be able to judge when each of those styles is most appropriate.
- Be able to plot your role and its current time demands using role amoeba technique, thereby increasing your understanding of your role and ability to make effective decisions about your use of time at work both now and in the future.
- Know the strengths and weaknesses of your management style and competencies and be able to identify how you want to develop in the future.
- Understand the importance of finding a mentor/listening ear, and be able to establish such a relationship(s) to help you talk through issues and concerns.
- Understand the importance of being clear about your values and principles, what is currently important for you both at work and personally in order to make decisions about the future for yourself and others.
- Understand the importance of making time for yourself – ensuring space for reflection, personal development, rest and respite. See your career in terms of all your life roles rather than just your paid employment.

# Further reading

Back, K. and Back, K. (1991) *Assertiveness at Work*, McGraw Hill.

Handy, C. (1994) *The Empty Raincoat*, Hutchinson.

Handy, C. (1989) *The Age of Unreason*, Arrow.

Harvey Jones, J. (1988) *Making it Happen: Reflections on Leadership*, Collins.

Hersey and Blanchard. (1992) *Management of Organisational Behaviour: Utilising Human Resources*, 4th Edition, Eagle Wood Cliffs, NJ; Prentice Hall.

Honey, P. and Mumford, A. (1986) *The Manual of Learning Styles,* 2nd Edition. Peter Honey, Maidenhead.

McGregor, D. (1960) *The Human Side of the Enterprise*, McGraw-Hill.

MCI. (1995) *Senior Management Standards*, Management Charter Initiative.

Super, D. (1981) *Career Development in Britain*, CRAC.

Woods, M. (1989) *The Aware Manager*, Element Books.

# Postscript

Not surprisingly, a book about change cannot, like its subject matter, ever end.
There will always be another chapter in what is a remorseless process. However,
the reader should not despair! This book will have helped you develop the skills
and capacities to manage that continuous process of change. At times your
organisation may simply flex and adapt in almost invisible ways to change.
Indeed part of the challenge is to create an organisation which can do just that.
At the same time fundamental strategic change typically requires a much bigger
response by the organisation and this book has sought to help you understand the
ways you might help your organisation to respond.

Looking ahead what can we see coming towards us which will bring further
pressure for major change? There are perhaps five issues to keep a close eye on.

First and close to home, the outcomes of the government's fundamental
spending reviews. Not only may the Housing review reform the shape of housing
subsidy but the Taxation and Benefit review and the Welfare to Work review
may reshape the structures related to the individual household. If one outcome is
to reduce revenue subsidy in the shape of housing benefit, the implications will
be far reaching and will require a major re-think by all housing organisations.

Second, Europe. Once a distant issue, this is getting ever closer. Discussion has
now turned to the housing market impacts of economic and monetary union and
this can be read across to private finance for social housing. There will be new
pressures regarding citizens' rights across Europe and again this will bring new
pressures in terms of the ways social housing organisations deal with actual and
potential tenants.

Third, disrepair, finance and low demand. Under-investment in the social
housing sector has been chronic. This has created pressures to lever in ever
larger amounts of private finance. The models for doing this remain very fluid
and new uncertainties are emerging not only in relation to the subsidy framework
but also in terms of long term demand pressures. Do we need this stock?

Fourth, new ways of working. Best Value principles, which will impact on both
local authorities and housing associations, will create a significant opportunity.

This opportunity is to utilise the challenges of companies and competition such that it engages those delivering services as well as merely imposing a discipline on the organisation. There is real potential for renewal, learning and innovation if it is utilised as more than yet another top down, imposed system.

Finally, yourself, your ability to deal with change. Your skills, your energy levels, your needs both personal and professional are all important.

# Index